# SECRET DETROIT

## A GUIDE TO THE WEIRD, WONDERFUL, AND OBSCURE

Karen Dybis

Copyright © 2018, Reedy Press, LLC
All rights reserved.
Reedy Press
PO Box 5131
St. Louis, MO 63139
www.reedypress.com

No part of this publication may be reproduced or transmitted in any form or by any means, electronic or mechanical, including photocopy, recording, or any information storage and retrieval system, without permission in writing from the publisher. Permissions may be sought directly from Reedy Press at the above mailing address or via our website at www.reedypress.com.

Library of Congress Control Number: 2017957316

ISBN: 9781681060750

Design by Jill Halpin

Printed in the United States of America
18 19 20 21 22    5 4 3 2 1

## DEDICATION

To Robin and Pete: Never stop exploring.

# CONTENTS

# INTRODUCTION

A city that is more than three hundred years old is bound to have some weird and wonderful people, places and things. Founder Antoine de la Mothe Cadillac, quite a character himself, sought a settlement near *le detroit*, or "the straits," because the land was fertile, the riverfront defendable and the climate pleasant.

All of these define Detroit, a city that has lived through countless ups and downs. It has enjoyed the highs of sports championships, architectural achievements and impressive progress, as well as incredible people who have made Detroit proud.

Yet it also is a city that has weathered riots, racial strife and the largest municipal bankruptcy in history. However, the 2013 reorganization gave Detroit its best hope to rebuild on a foundation of manufacturing muscle, resilient businesses, and resolute residents.

Detroit is full of secrets—but in the best way. So are Hamtramck and Highland Park, two cities within the city. For this book, secret is defined as something unusual, surprising or extraordinary. Detroit has plenty of all three.

Detroit is the kind of place that invades your heart and mind. You have to experience it—reading about it only whets your appetite. You have to get out there, meet people and see what the fuss is about. Everything here is sensory: Detroit begs for you to see, feel, touch, and taste. It is Motown music. It is coney dogs. It is Albert Kahn, Joe Louis, James Scott.

Never heard of that last guy? You soon will.

Detroiters are incredibly loyal, smart, creative people. During the past three centuries, they have developed a city full of pride, purpose, and potential. Many thanks to the residents who have kept Detroit going as well as the authors, historians and history buffs who made this book possible. Your knowledge of Detroit is as extraordinary as the city itself.

# 1 TOTALLY AWESOME READING DISPENSARY IN SOCIETY

**Who is a big enough Doctor Who fan to create his own TARDIS in Detroit?**

Think of it as the ultimate father-and-son bonding project. Dan Zemke called in his dad when he came up with a vision to build his own lending library for the public.

Zemke, who runs a local youth reading program called Reach-Out-and-Read, wanted a mini-library that would stand out at its Warren Avenue location. So the longtime Doctor Who fan came up with a novel idea: He would custom build a TARDIS to hold the volumes he wanted to share with the masses. With his dad's tools and insights, the two worked over the course of several months to put together their own police-box-turned-spaceship. Zemke and his pop constructed the ten-foot, one-ton behemoth to replicate the longtime British television show's iconic Time And Relative Dimension In Space time machine, or TARDIS. "We changed the name to Totally Awesome Reading Dispensary in Society," Zemke told the Detroit Free Press. "At first, I thought this was going to take about a month, but it unfolded into a much longer and awesome project."

## DETROIT TARDIS

**WHAT** A police box that holds books but also may have a secret entrance to a time-travel machine. No, wait, that's just for Doctor Who.

**WHERE** 1944 W Warren Ave.

**COST** Free

**PRO TIP** If you're heading to see the TARDIS, bring a book. Anyone is welcome to come take a book or leave one.

*The Doctor Who replica TARDIS—which holds new and used books the public is welcome to take home—is a landmark for the Woodbridge neighborhood.*

The bright blue TARDIS is an eye-grabbing sight, Zemke admits. He told interviewers he has seen people almost run off of the road when they catch a glimpse of it for the first time. But kids of all ages love the unique structure and the books found within.

---

**Upon learning about the Detroit TARDIS, history buffs at the venerable website Atlas Obscura declared Detroit "one of the dorkiest cities in America." Ouch.**

# 2 MOTHERHOUSE OF HEAT

**Where have generations of Detroiters gone to eat, meet, and enjoy the heat in the city's last steam bath?**

The Schvitz is an old-world tradition that found its way into Detroit culture around 1930. At least, that's the date written in tile around the cooling pool of Detroit's last remaining Schvitz. Detroit once had a sizable Jewish community, dating back to the mid-1800s. The Jewish middle class had a variety of businesses around the North End, Delray, and Black Bottom, or the Hastings Street area.

The Schvitz, which opened in 1918 as a community center of sorts, became a gathering space where men, women, and sometimes couples could relax, enjoy a sauna, and reconnect. A regular night at the Schvitz involved getting into a robe, prepping your skin with traditional oak-leaf bundles, talking to friends as you slowly sweated out the week's toxins, cooling in the pool, and doing it all over again after a drink and some food. It was

### THE SCHVITZ

**WHAT** An urban health club and the only historic bathhouse left in Detroit.

**WHERE** 8295 Oakland St.

**COST** Per session entry costs

**PRO TIP** There are separate nights for men and women as well as some co-ed events; make sure to call ahead to know what is available that day.

*"Schvitz" is a Yiddish word that means "sweat," and a place named after this term focuses on cleansing and purification via heat, steam, and saunas.*

*Detroit's last bathhouse recently gained new ownership and is undergoing a renovation to bring new membership and interest using Platza treatment, a holistic technique involving tapping the skin with oak leaves to release antitoxins and massaging essential oils onto the skin.*

said to be a regular hangout for the city's infamous Purple Gang, a group of Prohibition-era gangsters known for violence, rum-running, and their Jewish heritage. By the 1970s, the Schvitz gained a reputation for wild parties and its swingers scene. Its regular customers left, and the building began a decades-long decline.

In 2017, new owners began a renovation and reinvention of the Schvitz, noting that the city's revived Jewish population needs a place to gather, to enjoy natural therapies, and unwind in a safe and healthy space. The goal is to make the Schvitz a space where men and women can warm themselves in the sauna, enjoy the steam heat, cool off with a splash in the cold pool, and take in a meal together in a communal, spiritual way.

# 3 HUT SWEET HUT

**Why did a community of Quonset huts pop up northwest of the Corktown neighborhood?**

With Detroit's many demolitions and the resulting empty lots, large areas of land have become available for new developments. One such area that has seen a revitalization is True North, a group of nine Quonset huts.

The project, developed by Prince Concepts under the supervision of developer Philip Kafka, was inspired by the Quonset hut communities that popped up during and after World War II, especially in areas such as Berlin. For Detroit, Kafka and Prince Concepts wanted these live/work spaces to serve as private residences, but one hut also includes a gallery and another has rental units that are available as hotel rooms.

As you approach, the buildings appear as traditional Quonset huts with their shiny metal exteriors and semi-

## TRUE NORTH QUONSET HUTS

**WHAT** A live/work development of nine Quonset huts designed to serve as a community for creatives and visitors.

**WHERE** 4699 16th St.

**COST** Rental prices vary

**PRO TIP** If you want to stay the night, check out the units available for rent through Airbnb and other online hotel websites.

Architects modified True North's Quonset huts to make them longer and higher, making them more habitable and adaptable to a variety of uses.

*Developers wanted True North to serve as a quirky yet safe haven for its residents, artists, and hotel guests.*

circular shapes. However, the interiors are taller, larger, and more upscale, with tall windows, well-appointed kitchens, and large living spaces. Each hut ranges from 475 to 1,600 square feet in size. Prince Concepts also added new landscaping including wild grass, and thirty trees to the previously overgrown lots. To keep the units affordable, builders used readily available materials such as durable polycarbonate for most of the structures. The award-winning project is just one of Kafka's developments in the city; the former Texan is developing a variety of properties in Detroit, including a restaurant called Takoi.

# 4 A SPORTS FAN'S PARADISE

**Where can you see a baseball, football, hockey, and basketball stadium all within a few yards of one another?**

Detroit has always been known as a great sports town. Its four main sports teams are among some of the franchises with the most wins in their respective sports. The Detroit Tigers have won multiple World Series. The Red Wings hold Stanley Cup championships. The Detroit Pistons ruled the courts throughout its history, especially in the "Bad Boy" era of Isaiah Thomas and Joe Dumars. And the Detroit Lions? Well, their best years are (hopefully) ahead of them. But the one thing that also makes these four teams special is the location of their stadiums.

With the opening of Little Caesars Arena in September 2017, Detroit became the only city in America to house all four of its professional sports teams in a central district. As such, any fan can walk from Little Caesars (Red Wings, Detroit Pistons) to Ford Field (Detroit Lions) to Comerica Park (Detroit Tigers) to catch a game. Granted, not all of their seasons overlap, so you may never be able to attend all four teams' games within one day, a week, or even a month. But having all four teams in downtown Detroit is likely to

## FOUR SPORTS STADIUMS IN ONE CENTRAL DISTRICT

**WHAT** Detroit is the only city in America that has all four of its professional sports teams in a central district.

**WHERE** Little Caesars Arena, Ford Field, Comerica Park

**COST** Ticket prices vary

**PRO TIP** Arrive early to each of these stadiums on your first visit to soak in some of the sports history and legacies on display for the public.

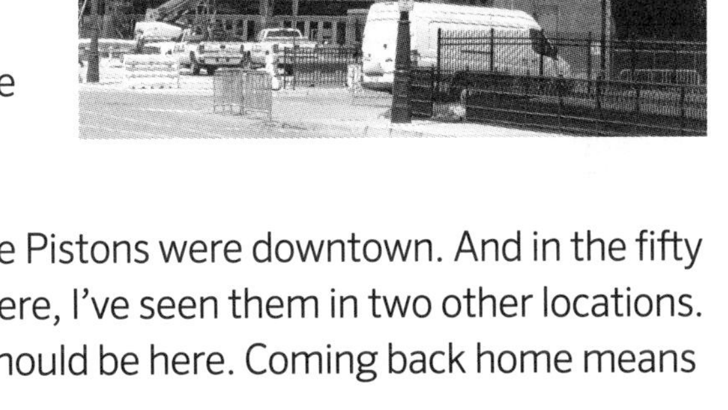


*Detroit team owners and, most importantly, its taxpayers have invested heavily in its sports teams and sports arenas.*

become an important economic boost for the city, its residents, and its sports dynasties. As former Mayor Dave Bing told the *Detroit Free Press*, "When I came here in 1966, the Pistons were downtown. And in the fifty years that I've been here, I've seen them in two other locations. I've always felt they should be here. Coming back home means a great thing."

---

**The Detroit Pistons once played at Cobo Arena—a golden moment especially because the team back then included Dave Bing, a former Detroit mayor and businessman.**

# 5 PRESS ON

**What musical artist loves vinyl and music history so much he put a record-production facility in Detroit?**

Michigan residents are generally huge fans of Jack White, the guitar behind the rough-and-ready sound of the White Stripes. White, who has become an acclaimed producer, wanted to bring his music label to Detroit. As a result, he opened Third Man Records in the Cass Corridor area (also known as Midtown) in 2015. Two years later, White boosted his investment in Detroit's music scene by adding a state-of-the-art vinyl record-production facility.

The facility makes Third Man Records the first label to have environmentally efficient pressing machinery in its climate-controlled pressing plant. As noted on the Third Man Records website, "each pressing station is outfitted with a digital touchscreen control for temperature,

## THIRD MAN RECORDS PRESSING PLANT

**WHAT** A record-manufacturing plant where Jack White preserves and highlights musicians of all eras and ages.

**WHERE** 441 W Canfield St.

**COST** Free

**PRO TIP** Third Man Records occasionally opens up the Pressing Plant for public tours; watch for times and dates to enjoy an awe-inspiring look at the process of making fresh vinyl.

---

*Jack White admired artist Robert Sestok so much he asked if the venerable artist would create a mural in the pressing facility. Sestok, of course, said yes.*

*Employees work with speed and precision to create records from raw materials shipped into the city for Third Man Records.*

hydraulic compression, and extruder speed, equaling increased control for the highly trained staff and a superior product." The records produced there preserve the work of new artists as well as historically relevant singers and songwriters. This is part of White's mission: to ensure that both local and nationally known artists are recognized and their work is preserved. At full speed, White's plant can press five thousand vinyl albums during an eight-hour shift with a cycle time of about forty-five seconds per record. The public can view records being made from the Third Man Records storefront, giving all music fans insight into what makes a vinyl record—and White himself—such standouts.

# 6 SHARE YOUR CANDY

**Why is there an art gallery in a vacant lot next door to a recycling center?**

Here are the directions to the Lincoln Street Art Park: Drive to Detroit's New Center area, just west of the U.S. 10 Highway. You'll find a recycling center along Holden Avenue. Drive toward the overpass that has these words painted onto it: "Danger: Reality Ahead." Look toward your left, and you'll see what some call the "Ghetto Louvre" or the Lincoln Street Art Park.

The Lincoln Street Art Park is best described as a non-traditional sculptural park built on a formerly abandoned industrial site. The park, which was created in 2011 through a Kickstarter campaign, is constantly acquiring new works

### LINCOLN STREET ART PARK

**WHAT** A pocket gallery where the public supplies art in the form of murals and sculptures for all generations to enjoy.

**WHERE** 5926 Lincoln St.

**COST** Free

**PRO TIP** You can schedule school field trips about recycling, sustainability, and our role in the environment in the art park through its educational arm known as Green Living Science.

---

Recycle Here! and its educational component, Green Living Science, are both dedicated to helping Detroit residents reduce their carbon footprint, reuse what they can (as art and otherwise), and recycle everything else.

*The Lincoln Street Art Park has transformed a once-empty urban lot into a hub of creativity and humanity where people sit, enjoy the artwork, and talk with their neighbors.*

of art when artists drop them off, sometimes in the middle of the night. It is bursting with color, and large installations and sculptures of monkeys, dinosaurs, and anything else an artist can imagine. Local artists, including John Sauvé (Man in the City) and Marianne Audrey Burrows have showpieces here. It is a refuge and a destination, a place where spontaneous parties break out and bonfires are a regular occurrence. The art and the resulting mood is primitive and freeing, giving license to creativity and expression. Every visit is unique and presents an opportunity to think about how Detroit could become more creative. And, as curator and Recycle Here! proprietor Matthew Naimi regularly says, "Share Your Candy" and be a part of the greater solution.

# 7 BRIGHT MINDS

**Why did the U.S. Patent and Trademark Office break tradition and open a branch in Detroit?**

With its research-orientated automotive industry, Detroit has a higher concentration of designers, engineers, and inventors than most large cities in the United States. As a result, in 2012 Detroit became the home of the first regional branch of the U.S. Patent and Trademark Office in the system's 227-year history. The Elijah J. McCoy Midwest Regional USPTO in Detroit serves the Midwest region including Illinois, Indiana, Iowa, Kentucky, Michigan, Minnesota, Missouri, Ohio, and Wisconsin. The office provides free outreach services for inventors, entrepreneurs, startups, researchers, and others interested in protecting their ideas and inventions. Specifically named in the America Invents Act, it is the first location the USPTO established to increase outreach, improve retention and recruitment of patent examiners, decrease the patent application backlog, and improve the quality of examination.

The office has been a rousing success, according to a spokesperson for the U.S. Patent and Trademark Office, who said that at the office's five-year mark it had granted roughly ten thousand patents in Detroit alone. The office

---

Elijah J. McCoy was the African American inventor whose work helped coin a familiar phrase. His name became synonymous with quality, and companies requested "The Real McCoy" to ensure they were getting the best product.

*The Detroit branch of the U.S. Patent and Trademark Office is open to the public for research and patent applications.*

is named after Canadian-born Elijah J. McCoy, who settled in Detroit and became a master of inventing out of necessity. He invented the folding ironing board to help his wife, a lawn sprinkler to improve lawn care, and a number of other practical items that people still use to this day. In 1820, he established the Elijah McCoy Manufacturing Company to sell his improved graphite lubricator. McCoy eventually became a U.S. citizen and held fifty-seven U.S. patents for inventions he created in Michigan.

## ELIJAH J. MCCOY MIDWEST REGIONAL U.S. PATENT AND TRADEMARK OFFICE

**WHAT** The first regional office in the U.S. patent system's 227-year history designed to increase community outreach, recruit new patent examiners and boost patent applications.

**WHERE** 300 River Place South, Ste. 2900

**COST** Free

**PRO TIP** You will need government-issued identification to enter the office, where you can research, ask questions, and/or start the patent process.

# 8 A TRIBUTE TO THE DEAD

**Where can you find a history of embalming fluid alongside burial records for some of Detroit's most famous?**

This is no ordinary college classroom. Open the door to the Wayne State University Mortuary Science Museum, and you'll see a century's worth of funeral history.

There is an arcane collection of caskets, embalming tools, medicine bags, religious iconography, and other materials used in the preparation of the human body for burial. There are the portable embalming kits that funeral directors of old carried with them as they traveled to clients' homes. There are cases of glass bottles with elaborate paper labels that once held embalming fluid and other chemicals used as part of the process. There also are books that show how funeral directors kept records of the services held at their facilities, documenting end-of-life

## WAYNE STATE UNIVERSITY MORTUARY SCIENCE MUSEUM

**WHAT** A collection of mortuary-science artifacts that illustrate the tools and practices used to bury the dead.

**WHERE** 5439 Woodward Ave.

**COST** Free

**PRO TIP** Call ahead to the WSU Mortuary Science department to schedule an appointment to view the museum.

*Wayne State University's Mortuary Science program includes a classroom, a laboratory, and practical instruction on everything from grief to conflict resolution to the psychology of death and dying.*

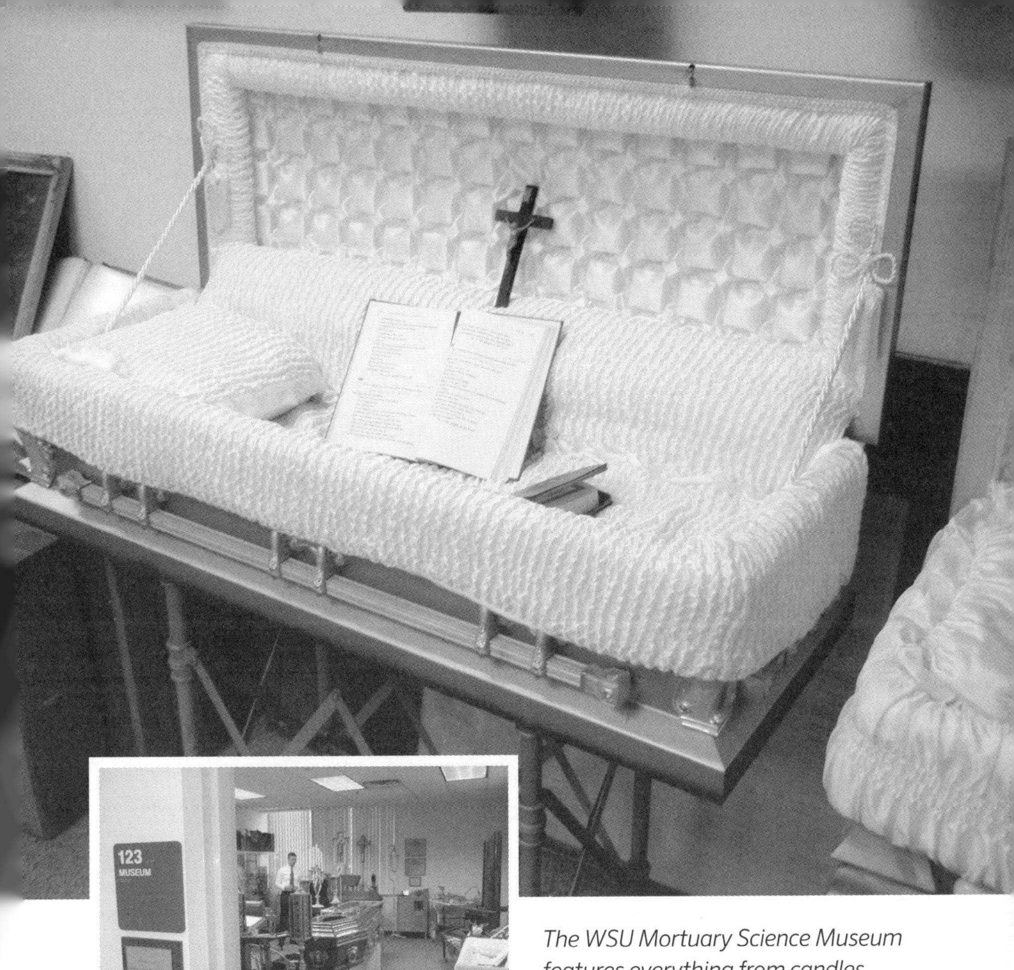


*The WSU Mortuary Science Museum features everything from candles to caskets to carrying cases for embalming equipment.*

traditions from Detroit's earliest history to today. According to Program Director Mark T. Evely, the Museum was developed in part because WSU Mortuary Science graduates donated items found in their funeral homes or from their personal collections. Today's students tour the museum as part of the curriculum, to learn about religious, social, and practical changes in the ways people have memorialized their dead in America's heartland throughout its relatively short history. Talking about death may not be easy, but learning about the process—both in terms of the science and the religious aspects surrounding the end of life—is fascinating in this well-organized museum.

# 9 STANDING STRONG

**What Detroit institution has the distinction of being the largest museum devoted to African American history in the country?**

Since he began working as an artist, Charles McGee has explored themes of unity, balance, and togetherness. His masterwork, *United We Stand*, is a twenty-foot by twenty-foot installation located on the grounds of the Charles H. Wright Museum of African American History. McGee had long hoped to be invited to place one of his works in the plaza next to the venerable museum, and he received the call to do so in 2016 when he was ninety-one years old. Using painted polychrome steel, McGee sought to portray Detroit as a multicultural city and to show the power of connection.

The result is a whimsical group of seven figures draped in black-and-white geometric shapes and patterns, each one seeming to dance to its own beat yet all moving as one. The installation is a feather in the cap of this world-class museum, which has been in its current facility since 1997. The museum's founder, Dr. Charles H. Wright, wanted to preserve African American

### *UNITED WE STAND* AND THE CHARLES H. WRIGHT MUSEUM OF AFRICAN AMERICAN HISTORY

**WHAT** Charles McGee's landmark sculpture, created as part of the Detroit 1967 riot/rebellion memorials, is one highlight of this large museum devoted to African American history.

**WHERE** 315 E Warren Ave.

**COST** Museum admission

**PRO TIP** After viewing the sculpture, take a trip inside the Charles H. Wright Museum of African American History to see its many exhibits or take part in one of its events.

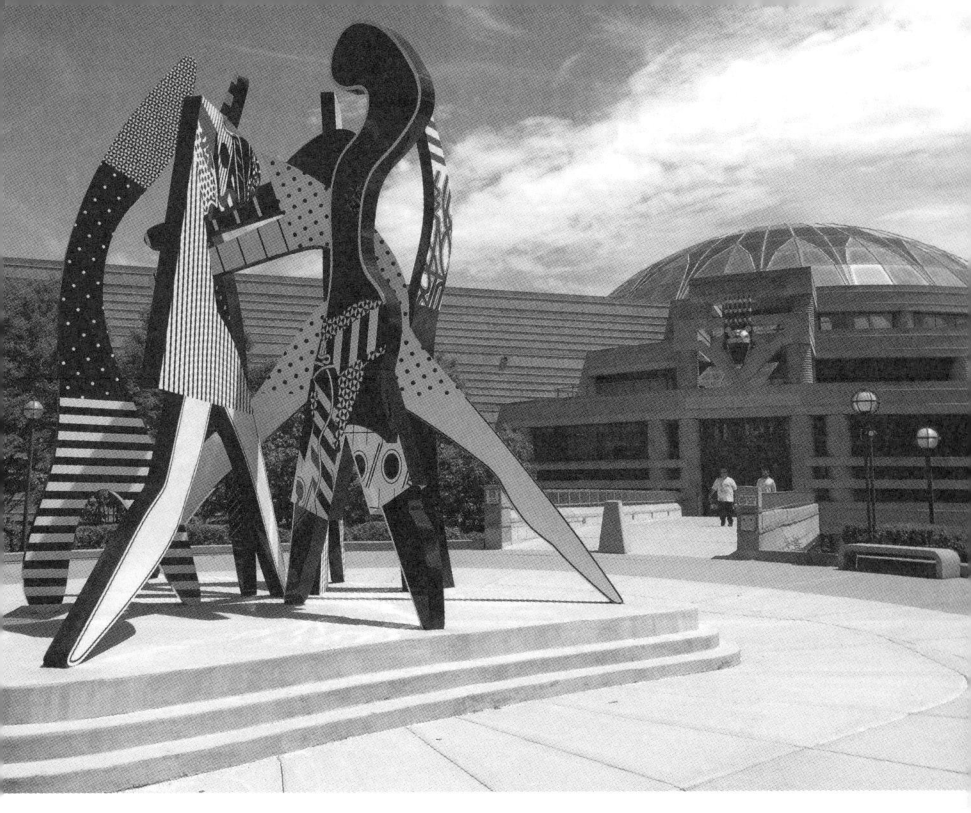

*Artist Charles McGee's sculpture serves as a "stunning beacon of hope" on the Wright Museum grounds, officials said at its dedication.*

artifacts, historical documents, and culture. The museum, which opened in 1965, has more than 35,000 items and documents inside its massive 125,000 square feet of space, making it the second largest African American historical museum in the world. Among its must-see exhibits are *And Still We Rise*, and the Ford Freedom Rotunda—a ninety-five-foot wide by sixty-five-foot high glass dome that is more than twice the width of the State Capitol dome and one foot shy of the width of the U.S. Capitol dome.

---

Other McGee pieces grace the Detroit Institute of Arts (Noah's Ark: Genesis and "Untitled"), the Broadway Station of the Detroit People Mover, and the 28 Grand building (a mega mural he designed in 2017).

# 10 TINY HOUSE COMMUNITY

**How could a neighborhood of tiny houses hope to end poverty and the cycle of homelessness in Detroit?**

When Rev. Faith Fowler heard of the tiny-house movement, she immediately knew that these small homes might be a good fit for her organization's mission. Fowler is the head of Cass Community Social Services, and she has worked with her staff, donors, and volunteers to eliminate the causes of homelessness within the city and beyond.

In 2016, Rev. Fowler built the first of twenty-five tiny homes on a piece of property next to her non-profit headquarters, announcing plans to rent these 250- to 400-square-foot homes to low-income Detroit residents. Anyone who remains in the home over seven years while paying for utilities and other costs will have the opportunity to own the home. Professional contractors assisted by volunteer teams build the homes. Each home sits on its own lot, living room, and bathroom as well as a front porch or back deck. Generally, they take about five weeks to build and cost an estimated $40,000 to $50,000 to construct. The homes' designs range from Modern to Victorian to Cape Cod, and their brightly colored siding,

### TINY HOUSE COMMUNITY

**WHAT** Cass Community Social Services constructed a tiny-house development on its Detroit campus as another way to help low-income individuals find long-term housing.

**WHERE** 564 Elmhurst St.

**COST** Free

**PRO TIP** Cass Community Services holds occasional fund-raising events that allow the public to view the interior of the tiny homes in exchange for a donation.

*The eclectic collection of tiny homes on the Cass Community Services campus is diverse on purpose to create pride of ownership among its residents.*

window shutters, and outdoor decorations make this tiny-house community a bright and cheerful subdivision. "Everything is very different on purpose so people have pride in their home," Fowler said in an interview.

---

Metro Detroit foundations, businesses, and community groups have raised money to help build the Cass Community Services tiny house development.

# 11 VERTICAL EL CAMINO

**What inspired a London-born artist to come to Detroit and install an iconic car perpendicular to the ground?**

It's been called "the most Detroit statue there ever was." And if you know anything of the Motor City—built on automotive ingenuity, sweat, and muscle—then you're likely to agree. London-based artist, filmmaker, and architect Anthony Gross came to Detroit in 2016 at the end of an epic cross-country, All-American ride he called "The Last Road Trip on Earth." Gross wanted to leave behind a piece of himself in tribute to his experiences on the road. The result was *Detroit Epitaph (Anthony's El Camino)*, a permanent installation on a former sugar factory site Gross purchased in a Detroit land auction. "It just felt like a good place to do an art piece, maybe a sculpture garden," Gross said in an interview.

On his website outlining the trip, Gross muses about the

### *DETROIT EPITAPH (ANTHONY'S EL CAMINO)*

**WHAT** A classic red El Camino that hovers perpendicular to an old loading dock from a former factory.

**WHERE** 1942 Alfred

**COST** Free

**PRO TIP** Bring along a camera to take selfies with the vehicle, Eastern Market's gorgeous murals, and the nearby graffiti of the Dequindre Cut Greenway.

---

If you love public art, check out the murals all around Eastern Market by some of the world's best-known graffiti artists.

*Anthony Gross and a team welded his road-tripping El Camino into a permanent sculpture and tribute to his American exploration.*

car itself: "The El Camino is this Powerful Object of Desire. How fantastic it is." Just outside Eastern Market on Alfred Street, Gross and the Flint-based Damned Wheel Club stripped the vehicle, hoisted his red El Camino into the air, pointed it toward the earth on top of a former dock, and welded it into place. The result is a gravity-defying monument to man, steel, and automotive excellence. Artists have since added their touch to the dock that secures the El Camino to the ground, creating an artistic statement of what happens when the road trip ends.

# 12 MAN ABOUT TOWN

**Who created the standout orange silhouettes of men found all over Detroit and nearby Windsor?**

You might see him along the Detroit riverfront. You may spy one staring down at you from the Scarab Club rooftop. He is the *Man in the City*, a sculpture project that artist John Sauvé began in 2008. Sauvé, who was born in Detroit, is an artist, arts educator, and public speaker. His art focuses on sculpture and printmaking, and his works have gained national as well as international attention.

Locally, Sauvé created several replicas of his iconic man-shaped silhouette/sculpture and placed them around Detroit, emphasizing rooftops. The goal, Sauvé says, is to create "a metaphor for life that transforms the skyline and encourages people to look around. In the discovery process, one becomes aware of their own sense of place within the City." At first, Sauvé placed a sculpture and let people slowly find it. Now, locals

### *MAN IN THE CITY*

**WHAT** Artist John Sauvé's international sculpture project found on rooftops across Detroit.

**WHERE** Locations vary

**COST** Free

**PRO TIP** Keep looking up. Chances are, you'll see a Man in the City mural or sculpture on a building near you soon enough.

John Sauvé also is the host of a television show where he interviews artists, authors, and creative people of all kinds in Metro Detroit.

*The fedora-wearing Man in the City sculptures are found on top of some of Detroit's finest buildings and rooftops.*

have made a game of seeking the sculptures out and posting them on social media. To date, there are more than sixty *Man in the City* installations in Detroit. Locations vary from Eastern Market to the former Packard automotive plant to the Grand River Creative Corridor. The Mark Ecko Foundation provided Sauvé with a grant in 2010 to expand the project into other locations, making it the first public sculpture exhibit to be installed on the High Line in New York City. Since then, Sauvé has installed other *Man in the City* works in other cities around Michigan and the rest of the country.

# 13 MOVIE MAGIC

**What theater has the state's largest continuously used American flag, indoor weather patterns and a ghost or two haunting it?**

Built in Detroit's most dynamic architectural period, the Redford Theatre is one of Detroit's last movie palaces. The Redford is what is known as an atmospheric theater, a design that emphasizes the sizable stage, exotic themes in its décor, and dramatic ceilings where hidden projectors recreate a moody cloudy night.

The Redford, a jewel in the theater portfolio of John H. Kunsky, lives among giants—such as the Fox Theatre—which served as entertainment palaces for Detroit's growing population, eager to escape the soot and heat of the city. It is a sophisticated old dame with its three-story grand foyer, velvet curtains and the state's largest continually flown American flag. The Redford got its distinctive looks, flexible design, and massive stage from the Detroit architectural firm of Vern, Wilhelm & Molby. Inside, its unique design with Japanese themes of delicate pagodas, mighty Mount Fuji paintings, feminine geisha girls, and menacing samurai says something of its era—although it would prove disastrous soon enough. By the early 1940s, the United States was at war with Japan, and all of those cherry

## THE REDFORD THEATRE

**WHAT** Various owners and a dedicated group of volunteers keep this dramatic movie and live-action theater with a gorgeous pipe organ open for business.

**WHERE** 17360 Lahser Rd.

**COST** Movie admission is $5

**PRO TIP** Try to sit up front in the theater—those are the newer seats with extra leg room to ensure guests enjoy the movie and the experience.

*The Redford Theatre features a Barton organ and the largest American flag in Michigan, as well as an atmospheric design that recreates a dramatic night sky on the inside ceiling.*

blossoms were eliminated by what eventually would be eight coats of paint. Over the past four decades, the Motor City Theatre Organ Society has led an all-volunteer effort to keep the Redford open to the public. They were drawn by its Barton organ, a golden goddess installed when it opened as the "Kunsky-Redford" in 1928. Year by year, dollar by dollar, volunteer by volunteer, more of the Redford's original elements are either found, replaced, reproduced, or created. Despite its age, the Redford has all of the latest technology, including a digital projector, the best in sound systems and high-end stage systems.

---

The Redford may be in a constant state of renovation, but it will always retain remnants of its past. The theater's original Carrier air conditioners—lovingly nicknamed Thelma and Louise—are still operational.

# 14 ARTISTIC AUTOGRAPHS

**Why would some of the world's most prolific artists sign their names on a ceiling beam?**

It is a beloved tradition that started in 1928. That is when a poet named Vachael Lindsey decided to do something radical during a visit to Detroit's premier artist hangout. On the second floor of the Scarab Club, Lindsey signed his name to one of the many beams that decorate the large meeting space. Since his bold signature appeared on the room's signature wooden beams, dozens of others artists have added their own names as well.

As a result, the Club's beams in the second-floor lounge have become what officials call "a living artifact, evolving over the years with the addition of each artist" who scribbles his or her signature. The Scarab Club now invites artists to sign its beams as a way to honor "their significant and lasting contributions to the arts." Signatures include

## SCARAB CLUB'S SECOND-FLOOR BEAMS

**WHAT** Artists of note have added their John Hancocks to the ceiling beams within this gathering space as a way to immortalize themselves and their work.

**WHERE** 217 Farnsworth St.

**COST** Free

**PRO TIP** Bring your magnifying glass—some of the signatures are challenging to find and are smaller than the artists' egos.

---

*The Scarab Club is one of the most unique wedding locations in Detroit with space in the garden and galleries for special occasions.*

*Artists—including Diego Rivera and Norman Rockwell—have signed the Scarab Club's lounge beams as a way of leaving their mark on Detroit.*

those of Norman Rockwell, Juliana Force, Marcel Duchamp, and Diego Rivera. The fact that these luminaries came together at the Scarab Club is why it is described as one of Michigan's finest venues for art, music, and literature. The Club, which was founded by artists and art lovers in 1907, sought to boost the arts within a city that seemed more focused on muscle and automotive might. Thanks to its inspiration, Detroiters have a place to meet, sketch, write, and create together where there are artist studios, galleries, and the inspirational beams. What artist-to-be wouldn't want to add his or her name to that impressive roster?

# 15 A CAUSE FOR PRESERVATION

**How did one Detroit neighborhood earn the illustrious title of "National Treasure?"**

A walk through the Jefferson-Chalmers District quickly shows how grand this historic neighborhood truly is. There are the well-preserved homes. There are the many storefronts—Jefferson-Chalmers is one of a few commercial districts within Detroit to survive the city's economic ups and downs, notes *Architectural Digest*. Then there is the grand dame of it all: The Vanity Ballroom, an Art Deco-meets-Aztec dance hall of rare beauty—despite its age—that once hosted greats like Duke Ellington and the Velvet Underground. That is why in 2016 the National Trust for Historic Preservation, along with Jefferson East Inc. and area preservationists, announced that the District had become a "National Treasure." This project was the first under the National Trust's ReUrbanism initiative, which focuses on how revitalizing residential neighborhoods can help boost an area's overall health, wealth, and sense of community.

According to Jefferson East Inc., Jefferson-Chalmers boasts more than 160 acres of riverfront parks, free boat launches, fishing access, and opportunities for outdoor recreation. Housing ranges from three-story mansions to modest ranch homes, while charming details like one-hundred-year-old brick streets continue to serve local traffic.

---

According to the National Trust for Historic Preservation, the Jefferson-Chalmers District was the first National Treasure designation within the city of Detroit.

*Murals, coffeehouses, and unique landmarks like the Vanity Ballroom are what make Jefferson-Chalmers a desirable district within Detroit.*

## JEFFERSON-CHALMERS BECOMES A "NATIONAL TREASURE"

**WHAT** The National Trust hopes to boost investment and interest in this historic neighborhood through this unique "ReUrbanism" initiative.

**WHERE** Corner of Jefferson and Chalmers on Detroit's East side

**COST** Free

**PRO TIP** Make sure to save room for some of the delicious food options popping up around Jefferson-Chalmers during its revitalization.

The neighborhood has recently received acclaim for innovative economic development strategies, historic apartment renovations, and successful pop-up businesses along East Jefferson Avenue. David J. Brown, executive vice president and chief preservation officer for the National Trust for Historic Preservation, noted that this National Treasure designation will boost this growing district and teach the rest of the country how to make preservation efforts like this work. He said, "We choose these Treasures very carefully, based on their importance to the communities in which they reside, the diverse stories they tell about our American past, and the ways we can work to make a positive difference in protecting them and keeping them thriving."

# 16 SITE D-23

**Where in Detroit can you enjoy an amazing view of Belle Isle and see the remains of an old Nike missile site?**

What is now known as Alfred Brush Ford Park in the Jefferson-Chalmers neighborhood formerly served as a radar installation for missiles stored underground on nearby Belle Isle. Back then, it was labeled Nike Missile Control Site D-23. The station, which operated during the Cold War, was deemed classified knowledge, and around the time of its construction in the 1950s, few people knew about its true purpose. As word got out and other threats became more pressing, the Nike missile station was closed.

All that remains today are several decommissioned towers that sit as a ghostly reminder of its former purpose. They are hulking concrete structures, some slightly cracking so you can see the rebar reinforcements on the inside. Other than these tall towers, there are no signs or indicators that tell the story of how Detroit was to be defended from a Russian attack post World War II. According to Nike historians, there were more Nike missile sites in Detroit, including Detroit City Airport and Fort Wayne. There were also other sites at Selfridge Air National Guard Base.

## NIKE MISSILE SYSTEM TOWERS AT ALFRED BRUSH FORD PARK

**WHAT** The remains of a defense strategy have become part of a large public park on Detroit's East side.

**WHERE** 100 Lenox St.

**COST** Free

**PRO TIP** Bring your fishing pole. Because of its quiet nature and reputation as a "forgotten Detroit treasure," Alfred Brush Ford Park is said to be great for fishing.

*Concrete towers are all that remain of this part of the Nike missile system, installations of which were located around Detroit, including those at City Airport and Belle Isle after World War II.*

---

The Nike missile project was a U.S. Army anti-aircraft system used across the United States. Nike is Greek for "Victory."

# 17 WATERFRONT POST OFFICE

**How did a small shipping company on the shores of the Detroit River earn the country's first floating postal zip code?**

The Detroit River is one of the busiest waterways in the nation, and the men and women who work on the tankers, barges, and ships enjoy getting mail like the rest of us. That is where the J. W. Westcott Company comes in. As the company is proud to boast, it has served the Port of Detroit with ship-to-shore service twenty-four hours a day and seven days a week during navigation season since 1874.

The "most reliable and dependable marine-delivery service on the Great Lakes" began when John Ward Westcott came up with the concept of sharing important information, including transmit destinations and dock documents, to boats along the river. Westcott himself rowed out to the vessels from a dock on Belle Isle. Using a rope and bucket, he could throw messages to the sailors. This process, called "mail in the pail," became a way to not only communicate but to bring items on board. Over time, its services grew to include delivery of just about

---

*James M. Hogan, great grandson of J. W. Westcott became president of the J. W. Westcott Company in 2010, maintaining the same family ownership for more than 140 years.*

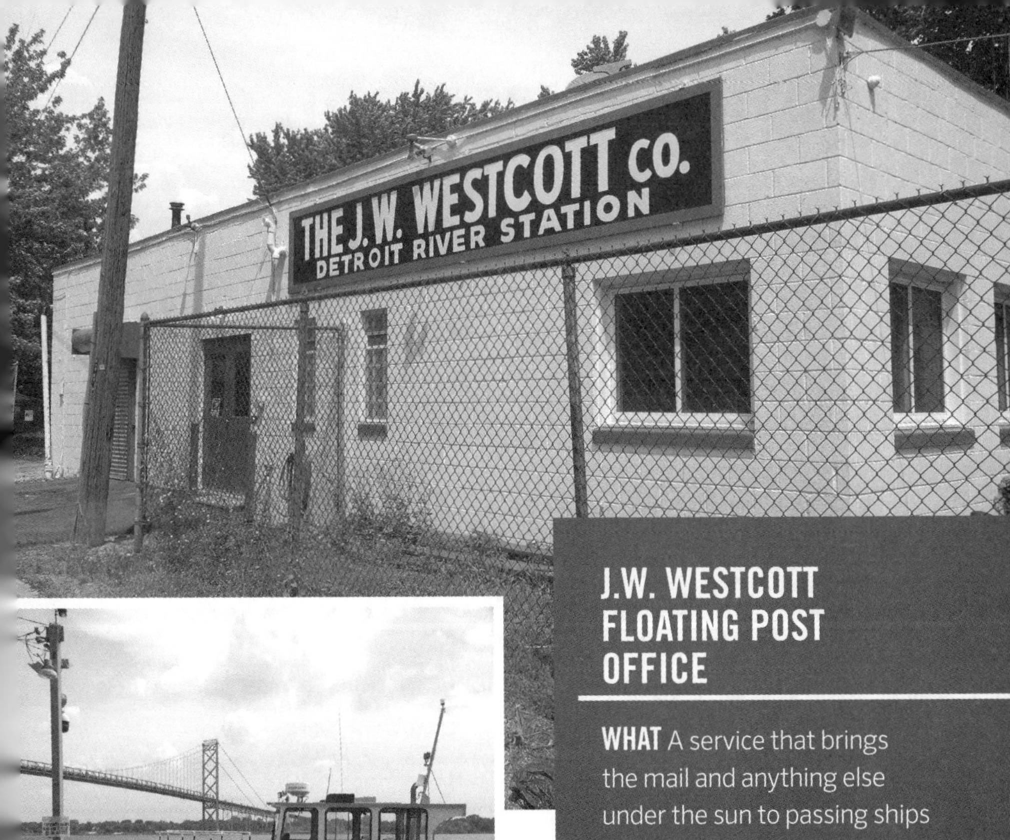


*The J. W. Westcott company uses a variety of ships to bring packages, medical equipment, and anything else passing sailors need to their ships straight from shore.*

## J.W. WESTCOTT FLOATING POST OFFICE

**WHAT** A service that brings the mail and anything else under the sun to passing ships under its own floating postal zip code.

**WHERE** 12 24th St.

**COST** Free (plus the price of postage)

**PRO TIP** You can send mail to any Great Lakes vessel via the J. W. Westcott using a special address with the vessel's name and "Marine Post Office, Detroit, Michigan, 48222."

anything from letters to pizza to flowers. As a result, the J. W. Westcott Company became the official U.S. Postal Service mail boat in 1948 and earned the world's first floating postal zip code: 48222. Known as the "7-11 of the Great Lakes," the J. W. Westcott delivers it all come rain, snow, sleet, or anything else that is thrown its way.

# 18 MARITIME MEMORIES

**Where can you see a famous anchor, walk through a luxurious steamer lounge, and feel like you're sailing a Great Lakes freighter–all in one museum?**

Detroit and its namesake river has one of the busiest waterways in the United States. Ships of all sizes have traveled its waters, and they have delivered countless shipments of goods to the people living here. Longtime boaters, the people of Michigan have a wide and varied maritime history, and the Dossin Great Lakes Museum is there to catalogue it all.

The museum features a number of notable exhibits, including the bow anchor of the ill-fated *Edmund Fitzgerald* and the pilot house of the scrapped *S.S. William Clay* Ford. Before the City of Detroit II. was scrapped in 1956, its opulent men's lounge—which

## DOSSIN GREAT LAKES MUSEUM

**WHAT** A maritime heritage museum that has artifacts from more than three hundred years of Great Lakes history on the shores of Detroit's historic Belle Isle.

**WHERE** 100 The Strand, Belle Isle

**COST** Admission is free

**PRO TIP** You can rent this waterfront museum for public events, giving your guests the run of this unique location along with dinner and drinks.

The museum houses former President Dwight D. Eisenhower's pen set, used to sign the agreement for the St. Lawrence Seaway. The pens were made from wood used in a Detroit stockade.

*An anchor from the* Edmund Fitzgerald *sits outside the Dossin Great Lakes Museum. Inside, you can find a Presidential desk set used to sign the St. Lawrence Seaway Act in 1954.*

now serves as the museum's dramatic entryway— once was a place where male passengers could gather aboard the vessel to smoke and have deep conversations over drinks. It is one of the most awe-inspiring structures around, with incredibly ornate wood, vibrant stained glass, and crystal chandeliers. It is a magnificent piece of architecture that wraps around three quarters of the room. After the Dossin Great Lakes Museum was built, local volunteers and maritime experts raised the funds to purchase the lounge, which is known as the Gothic Room. It needed massive restoration as it had been stored in an Ohio barn for more than a decade. But the result is a one-of-a-kind entry that is simply jaw-dropping.

# 19 THE GOOD DOCTOR

**Why are there benches memorializing a Detroit doctor at the busy intersection of East Grand and Gratiot Avenue?**

Detroit has long been a city struggling with racial discrimination, and its history of riots and rebellions is significant. Among Detroit's dramatic reminders of its violent past is a marble memorial that recalls a heroic doctor who tried to help people during the 1943 riot. From busy Gratiot Avenue, the rectangular stone memorial with stone benches on three sides simply looks like an unused sitting area in the middle of a traffic island. But if you come closer, you'll see a tribute to Dr. Joseph De Horatiis, a sixty-four-year-old Italian immigrant who had come to Black Bottom, a predominately African American neighborhood, to treat one of his patients.

Detroit Police warned the doctor to avoid the area because of the riot and unpredictable crowds. But Dr. De Horatiis is said to have waved off the police warnings, saying that he had a house call to complete. Soon after he pulled into the area, a rock hit the doctor on the head, and he crashed his vehicle. Rioters pulled him from his vehicle and beat him. His death shook an already enflamed city, especially those within the Italian-American community.

---

Dr. Joseph De Horatiis is one of thirty-four people who died during the 1943 race riot, which started after a patron at a local bar shouted that people were being killed at the Belle Isle bridge.

*A solitary memorial sits in one of Detroit's busiest intersections as a way to honor the life of a caring immigrant and unselfish doctor, Joseph De Horatiis.*

His friends and family pooled their money and purchased the memorial benches. At his funeral, one of Dr. De Horatiis's friends honored him with these words: "In his death Dr. De Horatiis offers a solution to all wars—Christian charity. When will the world learn that as long as men beat one another and strive greedily and selfishly against each other, peace cannot return to stay?"

## 1943 RIOT MEMORIAL BENCHES

**WHAT** Detroit's Italian-American community recalled the death of one of their own—Dr. Joseph De Horatiis, with memorial benches at East Grand and Gratiot Ave.

**WHERE** East Grand and Gratiot Ave. intersection

**COST** Free

**PRO TIP** Park your car and take a moment to sit at this somber memorial to ponder the effects of this riot and others on the city of Detroit.

# 20 RIOT OR REBELLION?

**How did a fight in one of Detroit's after-hours bars become one of the most horrific incidents in the city's history?**

It started as a police raid on an after-hours club at 12th and Clairmount. At around 3:30 a.m. on Sunday, July 23, 1967, Detroit's largely all-white police department began to arrest people at the club in an attempt to break up the event. The raid soon turned violent as nearby crowds became angry at the police, the situation, and what they perceived as a generally racist culture within the city itself. Fights, fires, and looting began afterward in the nearby neighborhoods of Virginia Park and LaSalle Gardens. Within days, forty-three people had died and hundreds of thousands of dollars in damage had been done to Detroit bars, restaurants, businesses, and homes.

Fast-forward to fifty years later, and Detroit is still trying to unravel what happened during those four horrific days. As the city approached the event's fiftieth anniversary, groups including the Detroit Historical Society and the Charles H. Wright Museum of African American History prepared exhibits and events to reflect on those frantic days. A historical marker was installed just west of Rosa Parks

## 1967 RIOT/REBELLION HISTORICAL MARKER

**WHAT** A monument to the location where the city's 1967 unrest began.

**WHERE** The intersection of Rosa Parks (formerly 12th) St. and Clairmount

**COST** Free

**PRO TIP** Gordon Park serves not only as home to the historical marker but as a "place of refuge for children who witnessed the riot first-hand," officials said during its dedication.

*The marker that notes where the 1967 conflict began and highlights how the National Guard had to be called in to stop the fires, looting, and property damage.*

(formerly known as 12th) Street within Gordon Park, which received a revamp in time for the dedication. The words, which begin on the south side of the marker and continue on the north side, talk about civil unrest, conflicts, and violence. But the words "riot," for those who saw the event as pure violence, and "rebellion," for those who saw it as civil unrest, are never mentioned.

---

**The historical marker highlighting where the 1967 riot or rebellion began in earnest was unveiled in Gordon Park in July 2017 to recall the event's fiftieth anniversary.**

# 21 THIS OLD HOUSE

### Where is the oldest house in Detroit and who built it?

The oldest documented house in Detroit has a storied history as diverse as the city itself. It started in 1826 when Charles C. Trowbridge purchased farmland at 1380 E. Jefferson Avenue. Detroit was a small farming community then, and Trowbridge likely saw value in its rich soil, its adjacency to the Detroit riverfront, and its proximity to what would eventually be downtown. Formerly known as Mullett Farm, the property cost Trowbridge about $2,500 to acquire, and he began work on a new home immediately.

The resulting structure was modest yet stately with two stories and several large windows. It served as a warm abode for Trowbridge and his family, who added Victorian elements to its exterior to update it. Trowbridge, who served as mayor of Detroit in 1833, lived in the house for fifty-six years and died in 1883. His daughters retained the building and turned it into a rooming house during the Great Depression before selling it in 1942. The next owner converted it back to a single-family home. Two owners later, the law firm of Grandelot, Stoepker, and Dickson (now known as the Trowbridge Law Firm) purchased the home and converted it to offices. The Trowbridge House was added to the National Register of Historic Places in May 1976 and was designated as part of a historic district by the city of Detroit in 1982.

---

*The original design of the Trowbridge House was Greek Revival, but various owners added Victorian elements over the years.*

*Banker and former Detroit Mayor Charles C. Trowbridge built a quality home that still stands today and is Detroit's oldest documented house.*

## CHARLES C. TROWBRIDGE HOUSE

**WHAT** The oldest documented house in the city of Detroit with a history that dates back to 1826.

**WHERE** 1380 E Jefferson Ave.

**COST** Free

**PRO TIP** Several excavations in and under the house resulted in a treasure trove of items that Wayne State University still has in its collection.

## 22 A USONIAN TREASURE

**What Frank Lloyd Wright house has the distinction of being the only two-story Usonian Automatic he ever designed?**

Dorothy Turkel, heiress to a parking-lot fortune, was a woman of refined taste. So when she wanted a home that would stand out in Detroit's upscale Palmer Woods subdivision, she reached out to the only man she thought was fit for the job: Frank Lloyd Wright. In 1955, Turkel wrote to Wright in hopes that he would design a home just for her. Wright took the commission, and he exercised his creative license to design Turkel's dream home. It has nineteen exterior doors and more than four hundred windows and adheres to his Usonian design aesthetic of simplicity and blending with nature.

The home looks like a Lego structure—the forty-three-thousand-square-foot house is composed of more than six thousand concrete blocks in thirty-six different patterns, held together with steel bars. The interior has a two-story living room, which Wright intended to serve as a music room. There's a long hallway to the kitchen, a den, and

### FRANK LLOYD WRIGHT-DESIGNED HOUSE

**WHAT** The Turkel House is the only home or building designed by Frank Lloyd Wright within the city of Detroit.

**WHERE** 2760 W Seven Mile Rd.

**COST** The price of a Palmer Woods annual tour ticket; without permission, you cannot enter this private residence.

**PRO TIP** While the interior of the home is stunning, the exterior and its exquisitely designed gardens by landscape architect Richard Hass are just as impressive.

*Frank Lloyd Wright designed this "L" shaped house towards the end of his career; it is one of the few in Michigan from the famous architect.*

an exterior terrace. According to historical records, the five-bedroom stunner cost $65,000 to design and $150,000 to build. Turkel lived in her famous house for twenty years before selling it to its second owner, who left it vacant for several years. In 2006, businessmen and longtime Palmer Woods residents Norm Silk and Dale Morgan purchased the home. They spent four years and a reported $1 million to restore it to its former glory, adding a stunning outdoor terrace and garden to complete Wright's design.

---

**Frank Lloyd Wright's "Usonian" style homes are typically a combination of glass, steel, and concrete.**

# 23 MUSICAL INSPIRATION

## How did Berry Gordy turn an $800 family loan into a music dynasty set in Detroit?

Berry Gordy had a vision of a world where Black artists received the same opportunities as those of the rest of the world. Gordy, a former Ford assembly-line worker, had several hits as a songwriter (Jackie Wilson's 1959 "Lonely Teardrops" is a prime example) and he wrote the kind of songs he wanted to hear on the radio. He also knew the kinds of voices he wanted to sing them. So with a family loan, Gordy rented a simple brick house where he lived and recorded his own musical creations with the help of talented collaborators.

Within a few years, "Hitsville USA" became home to the biggest singers of his and any generation: The Temptations, The Four Tops, Smokey Robinson and the Miracles, to name a few. In 1961, the Miracles released "Shop Around," and Motown's first platinum single put Gordy

### MOTOWN MUSEUM

**WHAT** A museum devoted to the people who created the Motown sound and recording labelfrom the 1950s through the early 2000s.

**WHERE** 2648 W Grand Blvd.

**COST** Admission for adults is $15

**PRO TIP** Do not bring a camera into the museum. Photography of the displays and collections is not permitted, even in the gift shop.

---

The wooden floor is worn out inside Recording Studio A as a result of producers tapping their feet to the music to the likes of Marvin Gaye and Stevie Wonder.

*The Motown Museum shows Berry Gordy's living space above his famous recording studio and highlights the instruments, outfits, and accessories its artists used in their polished performances.*

and his artists in front of an adoring public. Today, Gordy's investment has become the Motown Museum, a place where fans and artists of all kinds learn about how their favorite songs were made and recorded. Plus, the Museum has some of the finest memorabilia around, including Michael Jackson's sequined glove and hat. There are exhibits honoring the Jackson Five, Stevie Wonder, the Supremes, and the other huge talents that made Motown and its museum known across Metro Detroit and the world.

But it may not remain small for much longer: Museum management is in the midst of a multi-million dollar fund-raising campaign to expand its space and offerings.

# 24 A BELGIAN TRADITION

**Why would you throw a wooden wheel down a dirt track toward a feather sticking out of the ground?**

Just down the street from Grosse Pointe's tony mansions is an East side bar unlike any other. The Cadieux Café is home to its renowned steamed mussels, an array of Belgian beers that tell the tale of its ethnic history, and a unique game known as feather bowling. The goal of feather bowling is to get your roller—a thick, round hunk of wood that looks like a wheel of cheese—closest to the feather located on the opposite side of the alley.

According to legend, the game began in Flanders, a Belgian city where many people of Detroit's immigrant community left to come to Michigan in the 1920s. The Café's original owner set up the indoor lanes, and a semi-organized social club that combined feather bowling with good times began. These days, people of all ethnicities come together to try the sport, laughing as their oversized pucks go rolling down the curved dirt alleyways.

The team that gets its balls closest to the feather gets a point; the first team to reach ten points wins and has bragging rights. Even if you come for the live music or just to enjoy a pot of steaming mussels, you'll love this former Prohibition speakeasy for its casual atmosphere and great camaraderie.

## CADIEUX CAFÉ

**WHAT** A bar and restaurant that has one of the best sobriety tests ever created: Feather bowling.

**WHERE** 4300 Cadieux Rd.

**COST** Feather bowling lane rentals start at $25 an hour

**PRO TIP** Order a bucket of mussels to share with friends; the Cadieux is known for its tasty preparation of this steamed seafood.

*The Cadieux Café has the only sanctioned feather bowling lanes in the United States, so you have to come here to try out the real deal.*

---

In addition to feather bowling, the Cadieux Café once had rousing archery competitions. Imagine trying to shoot an arrow with a few Belgian beers under your belt.

# 25 POTATOES, SALT, AND OIL

**What is the longest-operating potato-chip company in the city of Detroit?**

In early 1931, a salesman named Cross Moceri asked a milkman named Peter Cipriano if he wanted to go into business making potato chips together. Cipriano agreed, and the two men began a partnership known as Cross and Peters on McDougall in Detroit. With its signature product selling under the name "Better Made," the business grew quickly, feeding the hunger of Detroit's sizable population of factory workers, weekend picnickers, and Sunday church goers.

Other potato chip companies sprang up alongside Better Made: New Era, Everkrisp, Krun-chee, Wolverine, Vita-Boy. Yet the combination of Better Made's cottonseed oil, fresh potatoes, and tasty seasonings won them loyal customers. As other

## BETTER MADE SNACK FOODS INC.

**WHAT** A potato-chip manufacturing facility that has been in business since August 1931.

**WHERE** 10148 Gratiot Ave.

**COST** Free (but you can buy chips from the factory store on site)

**PRO TIP** You can watch the potato chips and potato sticks being made from the front windows of the Better Made factory on Gratiot Ave.

*When it became available,
Better Made purchased the name "New Era,"
the moniker of its most bitter rival within
the chipping industry.*

*Better Made has manufactured its potato chips from its third location on Gratiot Avenue since the late 1940s.*

"chipreneurs" fell away, Better Made continued into a second and third generation of family owners, who are as devoted to the company's original recipe as Pete and Cross were.

Today, the company is known as Better Made Snack Foods, is still owned by the Cipriano family, and continues to manufacture its tasty potato chips, potato sticks, and popcorn from its state-of-the-art Gratiot Avenue facility. You can buy Better Made chips and snack foods at its small retail store which is decorated with historical potato chip tins and other Better Made memorabilia from over the years. A variety of other food products can be found exclusively at grocery stores throughout Michigan, supplied through Better Made's sizable distribution chain. Diehard chip fans can only get Better Made chips in the Great Lakes State unless friends and family are willing to ship them to those who are missing that salty goodness.

# 26 WE'RE IN THE MONEY

**What Detroit facility operates under the protection of a SWAT team and federal agents?**

One of the most secure buildings in Detroit—and perhaps the entire state of Michigan—is the Federal Reserve branch. Hidden in plain sight on a seventeen-acre parcel near I-75 and Eastern Market, the Detroit branch is about 240,000 square feet and cost around $100 million to build. The facility, which was built after the September 11 terrorist attacks, is 120 feet off of the road on all sides.

Don't try to come in without an appointment—the entryway's secret security measures can crush any vehicle that tries to enter without permission. The Federal Reserve also its own security dogs, a SWAT team, and a state-of-the-art shooting gallery as well as some of the best security equipment in the nation. There is good reason for such concern—there is a ton of money being stored in its impressive facilities. Its autonomous vault is five stories tall and can hold up to $132 billion. Its two cash-processing rooms have machines that can count 130,000 bills per hour. A pre-arranged tour of the facility shows off that processing prowess, giving an insight into how local banks receive their currency from the Federal Reserve. A team of economists also works there to help produce local economic forecasts as well as the well-known Beige Book, a summary and analysis of economic activity and conditions, prepared with the aid of reports from the district Federal Reserve Banks like the one in Detroit.

---

Detroit has had a Federal Reserve branch since March of 1918. It ranks as one of the nation's top five financial districts.

*The Detroit branch of the Federal Reserve Bank of Chicago has been on Warren Avenue since 2004 after leaving its original location at 160 W. Fort Street. The city's two newspapers now call that facility home.*

## DETROIT BRANCH OF THE FEDERAL RESERVE BANK OF CHICAGO

**WHAT** The Federal Reserve has a branch inside of Detroit that handles currency storage and processing as well as economic research and education.

**WHERE** 1600 E Warren Ave.

**COST** Free

**PRO TIP** One of the Federal Reserve's mandates is community outreach. As a result, you can set up tours of the Detroit branch by calling ahead and arrange for an appointment.

# 27 MIGHTY MASONS

**What building in Detroit has more than one thousand rooms and some of the largest party spaces in the city?**

At one time, Detroit had one of the largest populations of Masons in the United States. Therefore, it makes sense that the city's Masonic Temple is the largest building of its kind in the world.

The facility, which opened to the public in 1926, includes three theaters, eight lodge rooms, a 17,500-square-foot drill hall, two ballrooms, a cafeteria, dining rooms, a barber shop, and many other gathering spaces for a grand total of 1,037 rooms. Every lodge room has its own architectural theme such as Ionic, Doric, Egyptian, and Corinthian, and each one seems grander than the last. The building's details are stunning from its engravings to its marble installations to its ornate carvings in mahogany wood. Much of its grand design comes from its architect, George Mason, and his artistic collaborator, sculptor Corrado Parducci. Parducci, whose work is found throughout the city, is responsible for the decorative arches, huge medallions, plaster decorations, and elaborate chandeliers throughout the facility. Its grand chapel may be the pinnacle of the Masonic Temple's magnificence, and there is good reason why so many couples select this area for their weddings.

As interest in fraternal groups such as the Masons declined, so did local membership. As a result, the Masonic

---

One of the Masonic Temple's most touchy topics is the unfinished swimming pool on the sixth floor; the Masons ran out of money for the project and left it incomplete.

*The Masonic Temple, which became part of the National Historic Registry in 1980, is covered with art and themes highlighting the Masonic organization.*

Temple fell into decline and got behind on its taxes. Musician and favorite son Jack White paid the overdue bill, resulting in the building's management naming its famous theater after the former lead singer of the White Stripes. Its auditorium stage is the second largest in the United States, and its drill hall has a floating floor, one of only three left in the United States.

## MASONIC TEMPLE

**WHAT** A gigantic gathering space for Detroit's once sizable Mason community.

**WHERE** 500 Temple St.

**COST** Tours with a Masonic Temple docent are available many weekends for about $15 per person

**PRO TIP** Watch the Masonic Temple's website for its occasional "behind the scenes" tours that show off its unfinished pool, theater, and other private rooms.

# 28 AN AMERICAN DREAM

**Why would an ordinary homeowner create a kinetic sculpture on top of his garage?**

When people say art is subjective, they could be talking about what local residents call "Hamtramck Disneyland." For more than thirty years, a Ukrainian immigrant named Dmytro Szylak took everything that reminded him of his beloved United States—posters, photographs, classic Americana—and tied it together on top of the garages behind his Hamtramck home. The former General Motors employee created layer upon layer, adding music, lights, and sound to the growing structure.

The whole structure is an estimated 1,945 square feet, and when activated, it is a sea of sound and color. Some neighbors loved it and its honorable intentions. Others wished it—and the resulting

## HAMTRAMCK DISNEYLAND

**WHAT** An outdoor folk-art installation created by artist and homeowner Dmytro Szylak.

**WHERE** 12087 Klinger St., Hamtramck

**COST** Free

**PRO TIP** There is no formal viewing area for Hamtramck Disneyland, but driving into the alleyway between Sobieski and Klinger lets you pass by slowly. Parking isn't easy but you can sit and view it for a short time (as long as there's no one else coming down that alley!).

*Creator Dmytro Szylak continued working on his tribute to America until his death at ninety-two-years-old in 2015.*

*Two garages serve as the base for a folk-art piece full of found objects and hand-made items put together by homeowner Dmytro Szylak.*

crowds—would disappear. It may have started as Szylak's hobby during his retirement, but it soon grew to be his (and many other people's) obsession. At its height, hundreds of visitors would pass by, and noted fashion photographer Bruce Weber once did a photoshoot outside with model Kate Moss.

When Szylak passed away in 2015, a local group known as Hatch Art raised funds to purchase the home and help maintain Hamtramck Disneyland, and it remains in place as a tribute to one man's All-American ideas, his affection for his home, and his attachment to his adopted homeland.

# 29 EYE-CATCHING CAT

**What would motivate a local artist and his friends to build a cat statue as a neighborhood gateway?**

When Detroit's old Tiger Stadium was torn down, much of the infrastructure around it remained in place. That includes what was known as the Corktown Pedestrian Overpass, which once connected the city's neighborhoods and served as a pathway to the popular baseball stadium.

To beautify the area and create a new landmark, a group of friends got together through a Kickstarter campaign to build a giant cat-shaped structure as conceived by local artist Jerome Ferretti. More than fifty-five people raised about $1,500 to help offset the costs of constructing what became known as *Monumental Kitty*. Ferretti used about three thousand salvaged bricks to create his feline masterpiece.

## *MONUMENTAL KITTY*

**WHAT** A sculpture by artist Jerome Ferretti made of brick, gravel, and limestone in Detroit's Corktown neighborhood.

**WHERE** Cochrane exit near I-75

**COST** Free

**PRO TIP** Be prepared to park nearby and walk to where *Monumental Kitty* resides. It is near a vacant lot and busy freeway with no official parking area.

---

Corktown's abundance of cats as well as its proximity to the former Detroit Tigers' baseball stadium inspired artist Jerome Ferretti's installation.

*Monumental Kitty* greets people as they come in and out of Corktown, one of the city's oldest neighborhoods and biggest revitalizations.

The cat's head measures about nine feet in diameter and is about seven feet tall at the tips of its ears. It also has a small tail and paw nearby, waving to people as they come into or leave Corktown. Cats figure in a few of Ferretti's artworks, and the artist himself said he thought of the Sphinx when he was imagining what the *Monumental Kitty* might look like upon completion. Part of the project's inspiration also came from Loveland, a Detroit-based organization that began in part by selling inches of the city to people under the tagline, "We Should Own This." Now, a big cat statue owns a piece of Corktown's heart.

# 30 THE BOY GOVERNOR

**Why is Michigan's first governor entombed in one of Detroit's public parks downtown?**

Stevens Thomson Mason was known during his lifetime for many of his political accomplishments, including serving as Michigan's first governor, securing the state's border and establishing its statehood. His rise to power was swift. Mason's father, John T. Mason, became secretary of the Michigan territory in 1830 as an appointee of President Andrew Jackson.

When his father resigned from the position a year later, President Jackson appointed the nineteen-year-old Stevens to the job as secretary of the Michigan territory. Mason petitioned Congress to make Michigan a state, and he was named acting governor in 1834 at age twenty-two. Soon after, Michigan voters elected him governor. He won a second term as well. After losing the 1839 election, Mason left Michigan, moving to New York with his socialite wife. He died in January 1843 of pneumonia at the age of only thirty-one.

Although he was buried in New York, Mason's biographer successfully campaigned to have his remains moved to Michigan. State officials and family members supervised his funeral procession and burial in Detroit's small but tidy Capitol Square Park, the site of Michigan's first state capitol. In 1908, a full-size statute of Mason was placed over his

---

Stevens T. Mason was only twenty-two years old when he was appointed the full-time acting governor of Michigan in 1834. He was later elected to the position as well.

*This statue marks the place where the remains of Stevens T. Mason, affectionately known as Michigan's "Boy Governor," are interred in Detroit's Capitol Square Park.*

grave. The body was moved in 1955 and again in 2010, mostly because of new construction of a bus terminal and updated landscaping in Capitol Park. Today, its statue and state marker sit as a reminder of Mason's bravery and public service to downtown residents and workers who use the park for lunchtime picnics and social events.

## FINAL RESTING PLACE OF STEVENS T. MASON

**WHAT** After first being interred in New York, Michigan's first governor's grave was moved to a ceremonial location in Detroit's Capitol Park.

**WHERE** Griswold and Michigan Aves.

**COST** Free

**PRO TIP** Parking is challenging around the park, so be prepared to walk a short distance to the monument. The nearby park is small but well-appointed with benches and scenic vistas.

# 31 WOODWARD WAS HERE

**Where did Judge Augustus Woodward set the center of modern-day Detroit?**

When a devastating fire swept through Detroit in 1805, its public officials had lofty goals for how to rebuild the city. One of the most persuasive was Judge Augustus Woodward, who wanted to pattern the new Detroit on Washington D.C. Woodward found surveyors to set up a neat grid of lots, squares. parks, and streets that soon became known as the "Woodward Plan," which had a wheel-and-spoke design. The Canadian surveyors set up their equipment in what is known now as Campus Martius. From the park, they set the center point of the city and began determining its new layout from this location. It became known as Detroit's Point of Origin, and all mile roads are

## POINT OF ORIGIN

**WHAT** A street-level marker that highlights where Detroit set its centerpoint during its reconstruction in the 1820s.

**WHERE** 800 Woodward Ave. in Campus Martius Park between the fountain and the restaurant on site.

**COST** Free

**PRO TIP** As Campus Martius has developed, the Point of Origin marker has become smaller and less noticeable. Now, it is just a round cement marker near the doorway of the restaurant.

---

*The Point of Origin is located in Campus Martius, which means "Military Ground." It is named after an Ohio stockade and was originally used as a military training ground in the late 18th century.*

*Augustus Woodward and a team of surveyors set Detroit's Point of Origin where modern-day Campus Martius sits.*

named after their distance from this site. For hundreds of years, the original survey monument was buried seven feet down. Fast forward to when construction began in Campus Martius in an effort to revamp the park as a hub for downtown Detroit. Workers located a rectangular, six-foot-tall marker buried under the center line of Woodward Avenue. They carefully marked the spot, digging through all kinds of Detroit history including foundations, layers of pavement, creosote-soaked timbers and old streetcar rails. The Point of Origin resides in Campus Martius near its original location as a reminder of where Detroit started and a monument to one man's municipal aspirations.

# 32 GREAT LAKES LEGEND

**What makes the Livingstone Memorial Lighthouse so special in terms of its design and its material?**

William Livingstone was a legend in Detroit's maritime community. The former president of the Lake Carriers' Association helped gain federal funds to build the locks at Sault Ste. Marie, to further develop crucial waterways like Lake St. Clair, and to develop the Livingstone Channel. Following his death in 1925, Livingstone's friends came together with the idea of building a monument that would honor his life's work.

Famed Detroit architect Albert Kahn conceived of a dramatic lighthouse that would stand at the head of Belle Isle, facing Lake St. Clair. Sculptor Gaza Moroti came up with an Art Deco design for the fifty-eight-foot structure, which was erected in 1930. But what made the lighthouse truly stand out was the material chosen—Georgia marble—making it the only such lighthouse in North America made from the clean, white stone. The lighthouse, which cost about $100,000 at the time, generates a beacon that ships, sailors, and passersby can see for up to fifteen miles. Its goal is to help boats, freighters, and ships gliding along the Detroit River to find their way—something Livingstone

---

William Livingstone was the president of Detroit's Dime Bank, owner of the *Detroit Evening Journal*, and president of the Lake Carriers' Association, where he created the deep-water channel known as the Livingstone Channel.

*William Livingstone dedicated his life to Great Lakes shipping, and his colleagues raised funds to build a lighthouse on Belle Isle in his honor.*

fully focused on when he was alive. At its October 1930 dedication, H. S. King, Deputy Commissioner of Lighthouses, said, "The lighthouse has always seemed to me to be symbolic of two primary ideals, reliability and service, and that this permanent memorial has appropriately taken this shape well signifies the extent to which the life of Mr. Livingstone fulfilled these ideals."

## LIVINGSTONE MEMORIAL LIGHTHOUSE

**WHAT** A fluted lighthouse made of Georgia marble dedicated to a Great Lakes legend William Livingstone.

**WHERE** Belle Isle

**COST** Free

**PRO TIP** There is a parking lot near the lighthouse, but expect a walk to the lighthouse itself of about a mile.

# 33 HOW GREAT THOU ART

**What Detroit religious institution can boast that it was established two days after Antoine de la Mothe Cadillac landed in Detroit?**

Ste. Anne de Detroit is an awe-inspiring church for several reasons, starting with its founding date of July 26, 1701. It has baptismal, marriage, and death records dating back to 1704, making it the second-oldest parish in the United States.

In fact, from 1833 to 1844, Ste. Anne was the Cathedral Church of all of the Northwest, making it an epic landmark. In addition, Father Gabriel Richard served as Ste. Anne's pastor—the same man who published Michigan's first newspaper, co-founded the University of Michigan, and established Detroit's beloved motto: *Speramus meliora; resurget cineribus*. (We hope for better days; it shall rise from the ashes.) He celebrated mass at Ste. Anne's altar, and his tomb still rests inside. But when you add the grandeur, elegance, and dramatic presence of this building to its religious and historical significance, then you can grasp the meaning of this church to a city as old and as loyal as Detroit.

The current building dates back to 1886, and it is a grand example of Gothic-Revival style. Its sky-blue ceiling seems to touch the clouds themselves. The stained glass—some of the oldest in Detroit—has a glowing quality that makes the figures pictured there seem alive. Everything about this church, from its gargoyles to its flying buttresses to its incredibly active congregation, makes it a landmark for the city.

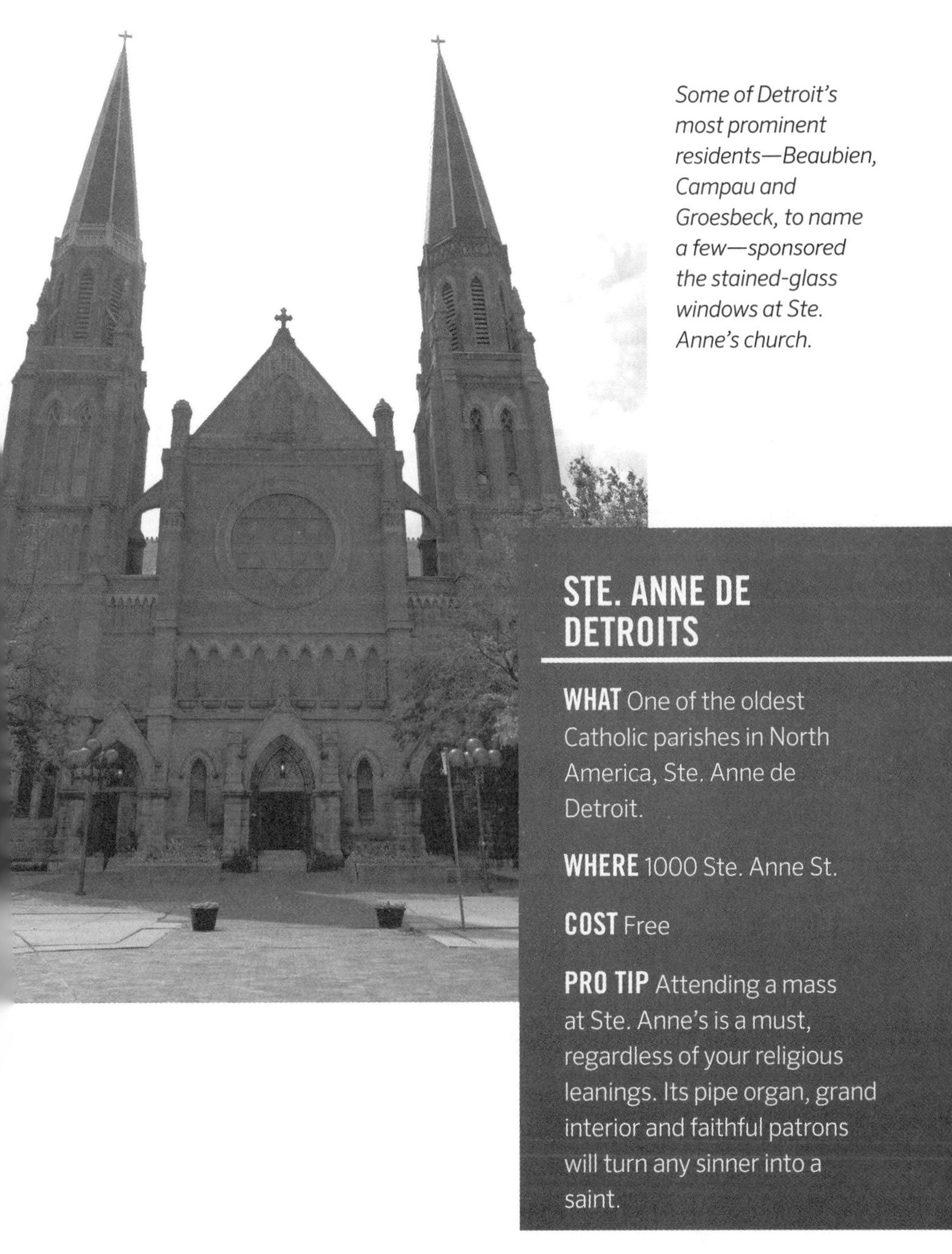

*Some of Detroit's most prominent residents—Beaubien, Campau and Groesbeck, to name a few—sponsored the stained-glass windows at Ste. Anne's church.*

## STE. ANNE DE DETROITS

**WHAT** One of the oldest Catholic parishes in North America, Ste. Anne de Detroit.

**WHERE** 1000 Ste. Anne St.

**COST** Free

**PRO TIP** Attending a mass at Ste. Anne's is a must, regardless of your religious leanings. Its pipe organ, grand interior and faithful patrons will turn any sinner into a saint.

---

Ste. Anne is considered the second-oldest continuously operating Roman Catholic Church in the United States.

# 34 SOUL OF THE SEA

**Where do sailors and their families go to honor their Great Lakes tradition and recall the loss of twenty-nine brave souls?**

It is a song that most every Michigan resident knows by heart: "The Wreck of the *Edmund Fitzgerald*." In its mournful lyrics, singer Gordon Lightfoot mentions a church were people gathered to pray for the twenty-nine sailors lost in that Great Lakes shipwreck. That religious institution is Mariners' Church. The song recalls the Nov. 11, 1975 event when the church's former rector, Bishop Richard Ingalls Sr., rang the church bell twenty-nine times in memory of each man who died in that tragic storm over Lake Superior.

The church, also known as Old Mariners' to locals, is housed in a white stone building along Jefferson Avenue. Inside its entryway,

## MARINERS' CHURCH

**WHAT** For more than 160 years, Mariners' Church has met the spiritual and temporal needs of the area's seafaring community.

**WHERE** 170 E Jefferson Ave.

**COST** Free

**PRO TIP** Check the church's schedule for its annual traditions including the Blessing of the Fleet, Navy League Sunday, and the Great Lakes Memorial Service.

---

At a whopping three thousand tons, Mariners' Church was moved nine hundred feet east to its current location in 1955 to make way for Cobo Center, the city's civic arena.

*A stained-glass window highlighting the* Edmund Fitzgerald *is one of the ways that congregation at Mariners' Church honors sailors and people who work on Detroit's waterways.*

you can see a stained-glass window dedicated to its maritime history and the *Edmund Fitzgerald* itself. Founded by Julia Anderson in 1842, Mariners' is part of the Anglican Communion and follows the 1928 *Book of Common Prayer.* The church has a unique history beyond the famous ballad. It is the only one in Michigan that is incorporated by the Michigan legislature through Act 142 of 1848. It was a stop on the Underground Railroad, likely because of its basement and location next to the Detroit River. And when the city expanded, the church was not bulldozed like any other old building would have been, it was lifted and moved across from Hart Plaza to make way for the city's growth.

# 35 LANDMARK SKYSCRAPER

**What did Detroit architect Minoru Yamasaki learn while creating what was known locally as the Michigan Consolidated Gas Company Building?**

Minoru Yamasaki is one of Detroit's favorite sons, an architect whose vision helped create the look of a growing city. He became world famous when his firm was selected to design the World Trade Center in New York, partly because of Yamasaki's work in Detroit and, specifically, for his work on what was known at the time of its construction as the Michigan Consolidated Gas Company Building.

The steel-framed skyscraper is Yamasaki's first major project, and it is literally built on a pedestal for aesthetic and design reasons. He did that because Yamasaki wanted the building to serve as a symbol of progress for the city as well as to highlight its height and power. Yet everything about the building also serves to meet Yamasaki's main design philosophy of "serenity and delight," or bringing peace and calm to its environment. The white, sleek façade is calming in a sea of other sizable buildings nearby. The vast, open foyer offers room to breathe and think. The windows, although small because of Yamasaki's well-known fear of heights, give a wide view of the waterfront and nearby landmarks. Moreover, Yamasaki rejected gaudy building names on the outside, leaving the exterior plain and simple. With its quiet pools and nearby statues, Consolidated Gas/One Woodward is an architectural gem.

*The lobby is surrounded by 82 glass panes, allowing for a wide view of the outside world for people coming and going from this large office tower.*

## CONSOLIDATED GAS/ ONE WOODWARD

**WHAT** A 32-story skyscraper that helped create Detroit's iconic skyline and became the model for Yamasaki's next great architectural achievement.

**WHERE** 1 Woodward Ave.

**COST** Free

**PRO TIP** Take note of the feminine sculpture in front of the building; Yamasaki regularly worked with sculptor Giacomo Manzu and asked him to work with him on this project. The female form resembling a ballerina is said to be modeled on Manzu's wife.

---

The reason the building's windows are so small is that Yamasaki was afraid of heights. He believed smaller windows made the skyscraper less intimidating for its inhabitants.

# 36 DETROIT'S LARGEST ART OBJECT

**What Albert Kahn masterpiece has a dazzling interior and more than 325,000 square feet of marble on its exterior?**

From every angle, the Fisher Building is a work of art. When it first opened in 1928, its tower was covered with gold-leaf faced tile, giving it the apt nickname of "The Golden Tower." It is an Art Deco landmark, and it always ends up on Top 10 lists of places to visit in Detroit for good reason. There are more than forty kinds of marble used on its exterior, making it the largest marble-clad commercial building in the world. The interior décor of frescoes, mosaics, and sculptures was created by Geza R. Maroti, who worked extensively with architect Albert Kahn to honor to United States' power and wealth. There are eagles everywhere with stunning tributes to American industry, agriculture, knowledge, and justice as well as an over-the-top Mayan-inspired theater inside.

The Fisher Brothers intended the building to be part of a larger campus, and the L-shaped Fisher Building was to be one of three. But the Depression got in the way of further construction and the plans had to be scrapped. Still, the Fisher building remains an architectural gem at 441 feet tall with 1.13 million square feet of floor space. It is connected to several other New Center buildings through underground passageways, which are still open today. The theater, storefronts, and interior remain vibrant, and the combination of new ownership and a renovation has the Fisher Building looking as good as it did when it first opened to the public.

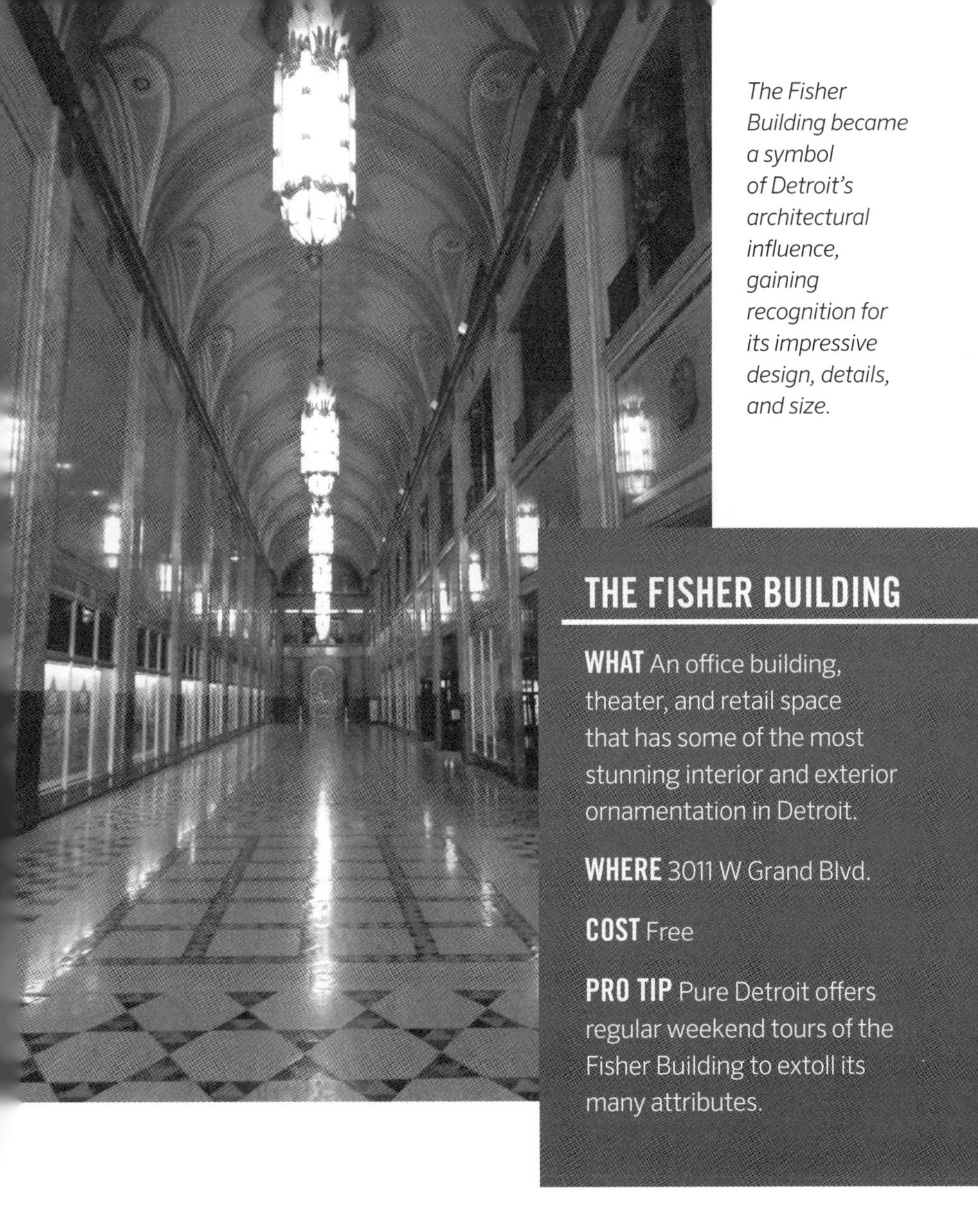

*The Fisher Building became a symbol of Detroit's architectural influence, gaining recognition for its impressive design, details, and size.*

## THE FISHER BUILDING

**WHAT** An office building, theater, and retail space that has some of the most stunning interior and exterior ornamentation in Detroit.

**WHERE** 3011 W Grand Blvd.

**COST** Free

**PRO TIP** Pure Detroit offers regular weekend tours of the Fisher Building to extoll its many attributes.

---

The seven Fisher brothers—Frederick, Charles, William, Lawrence, Edward, Alfred, and Howard—formed the Fisher Body Co. in 1908 and sold all of their interests in it between 1919 and 1925 for about $208 million.

# 37 BIG LEAGUE

**What city is fighting to preserve the last remaining Negro League stadium in the United States?**

Hamtramck Stadium is one of the last Negro Leagues stadiums left in existence. It may not look like much more than a steel skeleton and some wooden bleachers, but these remains mark the spot where some of baseball's greatest players showed off their skills. In its prime, the brick, steel, and concrete stadium was home to the Detroit Stars which included legends such as Norman "Turkey" Stearnes, who was posthumously inducted into Cooperstown in 2000.

Custom built in 1930 by team owner John Roesink for its proximity to Black Bottom, Paradise Valley, and Dodge Main, the stadium was home to the Detroit Stars and the Detroit Wolves, teams from

## HAMTRAMCK STADIUM

**WHAT** The metal-and-wood grandstand looks out over the field that stands behind Veterans Memorial Park and was a part of a Negro Leagues baseball stadium.

**WHERE** 3201 Dan St., Hamtramck

**COST** Free

**PRO TIP** Look for the murals on the nearby baseball dugouts; they tell the history of some of the players who graced this beautiful field.

---

*Hamtramck hopes to revitalize Historic Hamtramck Stadium to create a more active sports center for local youth; it earned a National Park Service grant in January 2017 to study the possibilities.*

*Hamtramck Stadium became part of the National Register of Historic Places in 2012. A state of Michigan Historic Marker was added two years later.*

the Negro Leagues that once played across the United States. The league's World Series, of sorts, was played in Hamtramck in 1930 with the Detroit Stars losing in game seven to the St. Louis team. Many traditional National Baseball Hall of Famers also played in the Hamtramck Stadium, including Satchel Paige. Tigers' baseball star Ty Cobb also threw out a ceremonial first pitch there as well. The city of Hamtramck acquired the stadium in 1940, but it hasn't been used since the 1990s. The segregation in baseball that required separate facilities ended in April 1947 when Jackie Robinson joined the Major Leagues; the last Negro League teams were disbanded sometime in the 1960s. Local historian Gary Gillette, along with city officials, led a charge to save and preserve the stadium in 2010, and their efforts continue in hopes of creating a new sports center for the next generations of baseball greats.

# 38 ROCK AND BOWL

**Where in Detroit can you find the nation's oldest active bowling center complete with sixteen lanes of bowling and a music stage?**

The Garden Bowl, a mainstay of Detroit's entertainment scene since 1913, is one of the oldest operating bowling alleys in the United States. During the economic boom of the 1920s, the Garden Bowl and bowling centers like it served as social clubs for middle-class men, giving them a place to gather, play, and drink.

The Garden Bowling Alley, which opened Aug. 1, 1913, was an entertainment palace with ten lanes, a billiards room, and a grandstand for high-profile tournaments on the second floor. Owners John Bauer and Irv Giese helped establish bowling as a popular sport in the city, and the Garden Bowling Alley was the first home of the Bowling Proprietors Association of America meetings. Bowling was one of Detroit's favorite activities, and the state still has one of the largest numbers of registered bowlers in the nation. Over the years, the Garden Recreation center served as a hub for working men and women—a place to gather, eat a warm meal, and hang out between shifts at nearby automotive factories. Different owners changed the building's configuration to add more lanes, a trophy shop, and the nearby Majestic Theatre to

## GARDEN BOWL

**WHAT** A longtime bowling alley and entertainment center that includes a theater, concert hall, and restaurant.

**WHERE** 4140 Woodward Ave.

**COST** Free, but there is a fee for bowling and concerts

**PRO TIP** The Magic Stick and the Majestic Theatre are ideal locations to see your favorite band in concert because of the venue's smaller size.

*The Garden Bowl, which celebrated its 100th anniversary in 2013, boasts that it is the oldest commercially operating bowling center in the country.*

allow more room for crowds and concerts. Today, the Garden Bowl has sixteen lanes with their original Brunswick machines ready for leagues, families, and parties of all kinds. The Garden Bowl is known throughout the city for its famous Rock-N-Bowl, a nighttime event where the lanes are specially lit and a DJ plays music from funk to punk to rock.

---

**Young men once served as the Garden Bowl's pin setters, putting each pin back in place by hand after every roll of the bowling ball.**

# 39 THE CATHEDRAL OF FINANCE

**What elaborately decorated Detroit office building is a temple to banking and finance?**

Detroit in the 1920s was growing in size and stature. With multiple industries— including automotive— thriving, the city had become an international commercial and manufacturing giant. A newly organized banking group called the Union Trust Company wanted to add its headquarters to this mix, so it began work on an office tower unlike any other.

When the Union Trust Building opened in 1929, it was one of the most significant Art Deco skyscrapers in the world. Forty stories tall and resembling an elaborate church, the building became known locally as the Cathedral of Finance. From the outside, its exterior has tangerine-colored bricks, a granite base, and terra cotta on the upper stories. The interior is very dramatic with a blend of Aztec, Native American, and Arts and Crafts styles. There are locally crafted Pewabic tiles lining the Griswold Street entrance. The lobby has a glass mosaic, and the banking hall has an Ezra Winter mural that showcases Michigan images in a burst of color. The steps and walls are Italian Travertine marble, and Monel metal divides the lobby from the ornate banking hall. Sadly, the Union Trust Company failed during the Great Depression, but investors saved it. It was reorganized as the Union Guardian Trust Company, giving the Guardian its name to this day.

*The Guardian Building's lobby and banking hall are visual stunners, providing a burst of color and eclectic décor that has delighted and impressed visitors since 1929.*

## THE GUARDIAN BUILDING

**WHAT** A Detroit office building known for its orange exterior of "Guardian bricks" and magnificent Art Deco interior.

**WHERE** 500 Griswold St.

**COST** Free

**PRO TIP** Pure Detroit offers informational tours about the Guardian from its store inside the banking hall area.

---

Wirt C. Rowland was the head designer at the architectural firm of Smith, Hinchman & Grylls, designing many of Detroit's most notable buildings including the Buhl and Jefferson Avenue Presbyterian Church.

# 40 WATERFRONT FOUNTAIN

**Why is there a memorial fountain named after a Detroit automotive pioneer in downtown?**

After World War II, Detroit and its leadership embarked on an array of civic improvements. One significant project was a two-level plaza along the riverfront at Woodward and Jefferson Avenues in downtown Detroit. The centerpiece is a $2 million fountain, named in honor of automotive genius Horace E. Dodge Sr. and his son. The city commissioned noted Japanese sculptor Isamu Noguchi to create the fountain and assist with the design of the entire plaza area. The fountain, which was installed in 1978, was intended to serve as a warm and welcoming attraction in the center of the waterfront park. The city asked for help to fund the fountain and Horace's widow, the heiress Anna Dodge, gave the city the money it needed for the memorial.

The Dodge Fountain is made from polished steel and features three hundred water jets programmed to spray water in a series of thirty-three patterns. Not only was the fountain a dramatic sight with its size and organic shape, but it also provided a water attraction for children and families during Detroit's warmer months. The finished plaza was called a "cultural landmark," helping to create public spaces for the city and a place for special events, civic proceedings, and everyday leisure. Named after Michigan Senator Philip A. Hart, the design of Hart Plaza remains one of Noguchi's

---

Horace E. Dodge Sr. and his brother, John, were Henry Ford's main suppliers and creators of the legendary Dodge car company which is now part of Chrysler Fiat.

*Noguchi designed the thirty-foot fountain with two inwardly canted supports and a stainless-steel ring suspended between them.*

largest outdoor works, a tribute to a city on the rise and its diverse population. The fountain, however, has proven challenging and is frequently in disrepair. Carhartt heiress Gretchen C. Valade in 2006 contributed to its rehabilitation, but even that has not fixed the fountain's recurring issues.

## HORACE E. DODGE AND SON MEMORIAL FOUNTAIN

**WHAT** A massive waterfront fountain dedicated to one of the founders of the Dodge Brothers automotive legacy.

**WHERE** Hart Plaza

**COST** Free

**PRO TIP** As you look at the Dodge Fountain, keep in mind what Noguchi pictured when he designed the water feature: "a fountain that would represent our times and relationship with the outer space."

# 41 GATE TO NOWHERE

**Why is there an elaborate gate along Jefferson Avenue and why doesn't it open?**

It may be one of the most ornate memorials in the city—a grand entrance to a park that few modern Detroiters have ever heard of or visited. But what an amazing piece of sculpture the Hurlbut Memorial Gate truly is. The Hurlbut Gate opened in 1894 as the front piece for Water Works Park, a 110-acre park that included the city's water filtration department and its equipment. Because of Detroit's heavy industry, the city itself was a rather dirty and odorous place.

Having green spaces like Belle Isle or Water Works Park was critical to the social lives of most city dwellers. Chauncey Hurlbut was no exception. The city business owner adored the parks in the city, and Water Works was among his favorites with its lagoons, floral clock, and swinging bridges. When he died in 1885, he included

## HURLBUT GATE

**WHAT** A Beaux Arts gateway into what once was known as Water Works Park along Jefferson Ave.

**WHERE** Corner of Jefferson Ave. and Cadillac Blvd.

**COST** Free

**PRO TIP** Look closely and you'll see the water troughs on the gate's front section for passing horses pulling carriages or being ridden by this popular resident and tourist destination.

---

*Water Works Park was formerly a wonderland with tennis courts, baseball diamonds, a library, greenhouse, and plenty of open space to roam.*

*The impressive Hurlbut Gate sits at the front of what was once known as Water Works Park, a huge public gathering space.*

money in his estate to go toward beautifying the park, and the city decided to create a front gate in his honor. The carved Bedford limestone edifice is dramatic and regal, filled with arches, angels, an eagle, garlands and other floral touches. However, concerns over water safety during wartimes and other incidents resulted in Detroit officials closing up Water Works Park, and the gate now sits at the front of a vast gated field. The Hurlbut Trust still helps maintain the structure, which has needed renovation and restoration over the years as a result of weather damage and vandalism.

# 42 FLORAL MASTERPIECE

**Why are the orchids housed inside Detroit's one and only conservatory so special to the city?**

With its massive glass dome, incredible array of floral life, and well-groomed grounds, the Anna Scripps Whitcomb Conservatory is one of the most often-visited landmarks on Belle Isle. Its history is significant as it is the nation's oldest continually operating conservatory. It also is significant because it is home to the largest municipally owned orchid collection in the United States. The Conservatory itself is an impressive piece of Detroit architecture, designed by Albert Kahn to resemble Thomas Jefferson's Monticello residence.

When it opened in August 1904, Kahn wowed audiences again with its 85-foot high dome, constructed in part by wood salvaged from the St. Louis World's Fair. A 1955 renovation replaced the wooden framework with more sturdy steel and aluminum. The Conservatory is part of a 13-acre campus that includes formal gardens, a lily pond, and the Levi Barbour fountain with a Marshall Fredericks statue of a rearing buck in the middle. The Conservatory's five wings house a wide variety of plant life, and visitors can delight in the many simulated climates that accommodate its leafy residents. Perhaps its most

## ANNA SCRIPPS WHITCOMB CONSERVATORY

**WHAT** The oldest continually running conservatory for orchids, palms, cacti and more in the United States.

**WHERE** 900 Inselruhe Ave.

**COST** Free

**PRO TIP** Weddings and special events can be scheduled on site through the Belle Isle Conservancy and the Michigan Department of Natural Resources, which manage Belle Isle.

*Many of the orchids on display in the Anna Scripps Whitcomb Conservatory came from her personal collection, which she created with the help of her master gardener William Crichton.*

impressive display is that of Anna Scripps Whitcomb's famous orchids. She and her gardener, William Crichton, bred these rare flowers at her Grosse Pointe home and donated a coterie of six hundred plants to the Conservatory after her death in 1953. The city renamed the Conservatory after her in 1955.

---

Anna Scripps Whitcomb is said to have saved many orchid varieties from destruction by sheltering them from the damage done during World War II.

# 43 A SECOND LIFE

**What turned a once-magnificent movie theater into a dramatically different parking garage?**

Your first visit to the Michigan Theatre will go something like this: You willingly pay a parking fee, receive directions to the third floor and dutifully drive upstairs. Next, let your jaw hit the steering wheel. It's that shocking when you first see the interior of this seemingly normal parking garage. That's because the Michigan Theatre parking garage once was home to an unbelievably beautiful movie palace that is stunning even now, nearly one hundred years after it originally opened.

When architects Cornelius W. and George L. Rapp created the Michigan, they put together an elegant 4,038-seat theater befitting the Jazz Age. Opening in 1925, the theater and attached office tower was the flagship of John H. Kunsky's delightful movie houses—opulent, romantic, and dramatic. It had a huge orchestra pit, a giant stage, and a Wurlitzer that could blow your hair back with its pipes. With the rise of television in the 1950s, theaters across Detroit saw their profit margins plummet, and the Michigan Theatre was closed and sold in March 1967. Several investors tried to revive the sizable structure into a club or rock venue, but they all failed. Finally, to satisfy the need for a nearby parking structure, the building's owners gutted the theater and added a three-level parking deck inside. Only a few original touches of the Michigan remain, but they are a glorious reminder of how movies were meant to be seen—with a touch of magic and majesty.

*All that remains of the original Michigan Theatre can still be seen if you go up to the third floor of this unusual parking garage.*

## MICHIGAN THEATRE PARKING GARAGE

**WHAT** A three-story parking garage put inside a former movie theater as grand as any ever built.

**WHERE** 220 Bagley Ave.

**COST** $10 for parking

**PRO TIP** Bring your camera because you'll need pictures to explain to anyone who has never been here how amazing the interior of a parking deck can be.

---

The Michigan Theatre was built on the former site of the building where automotive pioneer Henry Ford constructed his legendary quadricycle.

# 44 MASSIVE MACHINERY

**How did one of the largest automotive-producing plants go from cranking out more than 1.6 million cars to become Detroit's most infamous ruin?**

When it comes to understanding Detroit's automotive might, there is no better example than the Packard automotive campus. It started in 1903 and by World War II, the massive eighty-acre site along Grand Boulevard included eighty buildings and more than 3.5 million square feet of manufacturing space for boats, planes and, most importantly, cars.

Company President Henry Joy hired Detroit's noted architect Albert Kahn to design the factory complex, giving him ample land and inspiration. In hopes of improving employee morale and health, Kahn brought in his engineer brother, Julius, to design some of the buildings. The duo developed innovative techniques such as "The Kahn Bar," which reinforced concrete for strength, large windows for improved ventilation, and mushroom-shaped

## PACKARD AUTOMOTIVE PLANT

**WHAT** A massive complex devoted to producing the Packard automotive.

**WHERE** 1560 E Grand Blvd.

**COST** Free

**PRO TIP** Arte Express Detroit started offering tours of the privately held Packard plant through Pure Detroit in 2017.

*The Packard has a series of underground tunnels employees used as emergency shelter for drills and other evacuations.*

*Thanks to the creativity and engineering prowess of Albert and Julian Kahn, the Packard became known as one of the most innovative automotive-manufacturing facilities in Detroit.*

supports for higher ceilings. At its busiest, the plant had as many as forty thousand people working on site. The Packard plant closed in 1956, and the brand ended in 1958. The facility continued as a chemical company through 1999, but then Detroit condemned the deteriorating industrial park. It fell into disrepair, and it became one of the most infamous pieces of "ruin porn" in the city, drawing a mix of gangs, scrappers, and adventuresome photographers. In 2013, the plant's prospects changed dramatically when Peruvian businessman Fernando Palazuelo and Arte Express Detroit LLC bought the campus for $405,000 and began renovating it at an anticipated total cost of more than $40 million. The first tenants are expected to move into the administration building in 2018.

# 45 A READER'S PARADISE

**How did Detroit rate a public library with artwork, mosaics, statues, and exhibits that rival those in any museum?**

If books equal power, then the Detroit Public Library's main branch on Woodward Avenue is mighty indeed. By number of volumes , the Detroit Public Library system is the second largest in the state and 20th in the United States. The city received some of the funding to build its world-class system from library philanthropist Andrew Carnegie, and the facility opened in 1921. Cass Gilbert designed the main branch as a three-floor library in the Italian Renaissance style complete with bronze, marble, Pewabic tile, and intricate wood carvings throughout the building. Gilbert, who also designed the U.S. Supreme Court building in Washington D.C., added Greek and Roman motifs highlighting wisdom and knowledge.

The building's interior has many eye-popping details, including the Grand Staircase, the Shakespeare mosaics in the Fine Arts room, and a children's room with a Pewabic fireplace. Among its murals are epic scenes from artist Gari Melcher, who highlights the early settling of the city, including the arrival of Antoine del la Mothe Cadillac on the Detroit River and the uprising of the Ottawa war-leader, Pontiac. As its collection paralleled the city's growth, the

---

Architect Cass Gilbert had the words "Knowledge is Power" carved into marble to hang above the main Woodward Avenue entrance.

The Detroit Public Library is one of the most dramatically beautiful ornamented buildings in the city with a collection of world-class art and rare books.

## DETROIT PUBLIC LIBRARY

**WHAT** A researcher's dream collection of art, books, and historical documents.

**WHERE** 5201 Woodward Ave.

**COST** Free

**PRO TIP** The Detroit Public Library's Friends group offers regular tours to show off its art collection and architectural beauty; sign up for a tour for a small donation.

library added two additional wings to hold books as well as artwork. One of the most stunning additions is *Man's Mobility*, a soaring triptych on the west wall of Adam Strohm Hall painted by local artist John Stephens Coppin in 1965. There are other treasures sprinkled throughout, including a chest that once belonged to Russian leader Joseph Stalin.

# 46 MODERN LOVE

**What happens when you turn a former automotive dealership into an innovative contemporary art museum?**

From its bold exterior murals to the experimental art inside, the Museum of Contemporary Art Detroit is a wonder. What started as an automotive dealership turned storage facility has become a twenty-two-thousand-square-foot art mecca where some of today's most talented artists can show their work. MOCAD started its life as Standard Auto Company when the owners wanted a showplace for Detroit's car manufacturers.

When it was under construction, a 1907 *Detroit Free Press* article about the building bragged that the new garage would be the "most elaborate structure of its kind in the city." Architects Albert Kahn and Ernest Willoughby wanted to make it "one of the finest garages in the West" and gave "careful consideration ... in designing and placing the building to have it harmonize with the surrounding property." During its renovation in 1995, creators Marsha Miro, art critic for the *Detroit Free Press*, and the late Susanne Hilberry, a revered gallery owner, kept the space's urbane feel, leaving its rooms raw and cavernous. Their goal was to create a place

## MOCAD

**WHAT** A contemporary art museum housed in a former automotive dealership and repair shop.

**WHERE** 4454 Woodward Ave.

**COST** Suggested $5 per person

**PRO TIP** Be sure to check out the museum's permanent exhibit next door—Mike Kelley's *Mobile Homestead*, a full-scale replica of the single-story ranch house in which artist and hometown boy Kelley grew up.

*Detroit architect Andrew Zago integrated the old and the new needs for the space when he led the renovation of a former auto dealership into a contemporary art museum.*

where contemporary artists could thrive and develop the city's cultural core during a time of disinvestment. It still fits in well with its neighborhood, especially given its proximity to Detroit's art and music centers, the Detroit Symphony Orchestra and the Detroit Institute of Arts. Today, MOCAD brings visitors from across the globe to its door to see the art world's contemporary masters. Visitors of all ages appreciate its open space with large windows. Patrons can also enjoy the regular lectures, film showings, literary readings and musical performances after which they can stop for coffee, pastries, lunch or a happy hour amid the art at the Café 78.

---

**Detroit architect Andrew Zago integrated the old and the new needs for the space when he led the renovation of a former auto dealership into a contemporary art museum.**

# 47 A TIMELY LANDMARK

**What inspired Detroiters to turn a timepiece into a community landmark that has stood the test of time?**

When Ernst Kern built his department store in downtown Detroit, he wanted something at the entrance that would catch people's attention. In 1933, he installed a clock which was iconic enough to inspire generations of Detroiters to direct family and friends to "meet under the Kern's Clock" when shopping downtown.

Kern's quickly became a beloved retailer, pioneering delivery of its goods by mail and other shopping conveniences. By the late 1950s, however, residential changes resulted in Kern's closing and the clock going into storage when the building was demolished in 1966. Several community groups tried to bring the clock back only to have it removed again to avoid being demolished with another department store,

## KERN'S CLOCK

**WHAT** A distinctive clock that Detroiters counted on to keep time and provide an easily recognizable meeting place while shopping in downtown Detroit.

**WHERE** Corner of Gratiot and Woodward Aves.

**COST** Free

**PRO TIP** The Kern's Clock is an ideal landmark for meeting family and friends in the downtown area because of its proximity to parks, stores, and parking.

---

*The Ernst Kern Company Department store, which stands at the corner of Woodward and Gratiot, was founded in 1883 by Ernst Kern Sr. and his wife, Marie Held Kern.*

*One of the Henry Ford Museum's top curators refurbished the clock in 2003 for the Compuware building.*

the venerable Hudson's building. The third time was the charm for the Kern's clock. In 2003, the Compuware Corporation brought the beloved timepiece back to its original location and reinstalled it outside its headquarters. Today, it stands in the middle of a retail renaissance for downtown Detroit with signature Detroit brands like Avalon Bread joining national chains such as Nike along the Woodward corridor. People still meet at the Kern's Clock and rely on it to keep Detroit moving forward in a timely fashion.

# 48 COUNTRY ESTATE

**Why is there a log cabin in the middle of one of Detroit's largest parks?**

As you cruise through Detroit's Palmer Park, you'll see the normal installations such as slides, swings, baseball diamonds, and ... a log cabin? Built in 1885, the Palmer Log Cabin is indeed an integral part of this municipal space dedicated to family recreation and gatherings.

The cabin is named after the couple that built it—Senator Thomas Palmer and his wife Elizabeth Merrill Palmer. Both were longtime Detroit residents; he made his money in real estate and lumber. Elizabeth Palmer asked her husband for a log house, thinking it and the wooded property they owned would provide an escape from city life. The exterior of the two-story cabin is deceiving—inside, it is a traditional Victorian-style home with all of the modern conveniences

## PALMER PARK LOG CABIN

**WHAT** A former Senator's summer retreat turned into a historical site for visitors to Palmer Park.

**WHERE** 910 Merrill Plaisance

**COST** Free but donations accepted

**PRO TIP** The People for Palmer Park, a group of dedicated residents and supporters, hold regular fund-raising events for the Log Cabin on the property and open it up for tours.

*The log cabin's architects—George D. Mason and Zachariah Rice—were mentors to beloved Detroit architect Albert Kahn, known for his factory designs.*

*The Palmer Park Log Cabin was once surrounded by orchards, and the Palmer family made cider for family and friends from the apples the trees produced.*

of the time, wrapped in a log veneer. The Palmers used the cabin and nearby orchards to entertain a variety of friends, families, and local dignitaries. Senator Palmer was particularly proud of the nearby farm, where he kept his Percheron horses and Jersey cows. Senator Palmer donated the cabin and 140 acres of his sizable estate to the city in 1893 with the stipulation that the land remain untouched. In 1897, the city named the new park after the senator as thanks. The cabin remained popular for decades but was closed in the 1970s due to the need for repairs. Recently, the city of Detroit along with nearby residents of the upscale Palmer Park subdivision, have invested heavily in the log cabin, installing a new cedar shake roof, stabilizing the foundation, rehabbing the windows, and filling in the mortar between the exterior wood logs so the cabin can last well into future generations.

# 49 MAN VERSUS MOB

**How did a Detroit doctor become part of a murder trial because of where he chose to buy a home?**

For decades, there were unwritten as well as written laws that governed where Black people could live in Detroit. These covenants dictated the neighborhoods deemed acceptable for Blacks versus those "reserved" for whites. In 1925, Dr. Ossian Sweet, a Black physician, and his wife, Gladys, found a one-and-a-half story brick house that they fell in love with and purchased. Dr. Sweet wanted the home despite the covenants on it because he wanted a better life for his family. However, it was in an all-white neighborhood and neighbors were angry when they saw the Sweets moving in.

Despite police protection, a mob surrounded the home to harass the Sweets on the night of September 9, 1925. Dr. Sweet called on friends to come and defend his new home. When the white mob rushed the home, one of Sweet's friends shot into the crowd from an upstairs window. One man was killed and another seriously hurt. Dr. Sweet and several of his friends were arrested and the prosecutor charged them with first-degree murder.

The Detroit-based trial gained national attention when the National Association for the Advancement of Colored People brought in famous attorney Clarence Darrow to defend Dr. Sweet. A jury came back without a verdict, and

---

Dr. Ossian Sweet was a graduate of Howard University Medical School and came to Detroit to work at Dunbar Hospital, a medical facility open to Blacks.

Dr. Ossian Sweet rented his home to a white family until 1930, when he moved into the home. He sold it in 1946 to move into an apartment above his business.

## OSSIAN SWEET HOUSE

**WHAT** The home where a Black doctor had to defend himself against a white mob that was angry he had moved into the neighborhood.

**WHERE** 2905 Garland Rd.

**COST** Free

**PRO TIP** Because the Sweet home is a private residence, tours are not available and the property is not open to the public.

Judge Frank Murphy declared a mistrial. A second trial came back in an acquittal. The Sweet home sits at the end of its block—an impressive and cozy residence any family would be proud to own. The Ossian Sweet House was designated as a Michigan State Historic Site in 1975, and it was listed on the National Register of Historic Places in 1985.

# 50 BEADS AS ART

**What inspired an artist to turn an otherwise vacant space into a one-of-a-kind museum and outdoor art park?**

The moment the MBAD African Bead Museum and neighboring art park comes into view, you know you have been transported into an artist's vision of the world in one city block. Using mirrored murals, bright beads, and a variety of found materials to create African motifs and patterns, Olayami Dabls has created a portrait of the people, places, and lands he loves. Dabls was a curator and artist-in-residence at the Charles H. Wright Museum of African American History, which inspired him to create the African Bead Museum and sculpture garden.

Dabls opened the museum and retail store in 1994 to both inspire the community and honor what he sees as the beauty and wisdom of African culture. Dabls, a noted artist, has collected an array of African artifacts, including pottery, textiles, sculptures, and beads, some of which date back as far as four hundred years. People visit the African Bead Gallery, N'kisi House, and the African Language Wall, purchase beads hand-crafted from across Africa for their own creations and tour the neighboring outdoor art installations, many of which were created by Dabls himself. Kresge Arts in Detroit, which awarded Dabls a visual-arts grant in 2011 to expand his project to nearby lots, described

---

Olayami Dabls describes himself as a visual storyteller who works in a wide range of materials such as iron, rock, wood, and mirrors to create his large installations.

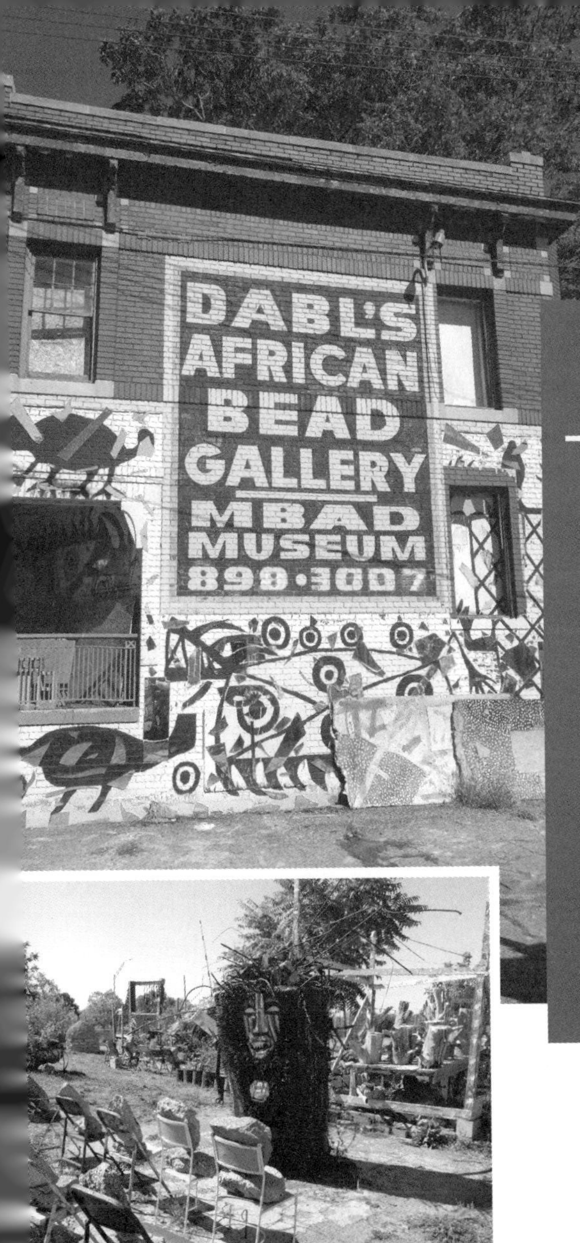


*The MBAD African Bead Museum offers a look into the craftmanship and integrity of African artists.*

## MBAD AFRICAN BEAD MUSEUM

**WHAT** A business and community-gathering spot with a rare bead museum, outdoor art installations, and a retail store.

**WHERE** 6559 Grand River Ave.

**COST** Free

**PRO TIP** Call ahead to make sure the Bead Museum is open; Dabls is always busy making something and may not be on site depending on when you visit.

his work as telling stories "about African people in particular and about Africa's material culture embodying his ancestor history, mythology, creation myths, systems of thought, and philosophy." Dabls has created a place of history, culture, and energy where people of all ages, ethnicities, and cultural backgrounds can learn about Africa, African art, and African culture.

# 51 A MODERNIST VIEW

**How did one of the last century's greatest architects turn a Detroit development into his vision of a utopian neighborhood?**

Imagine an urban oasis filled with trees, lush plantings, and architecture that blends into the landscape. That is Lafayette Park, a forty-six-acre residential development that is modern yet traditional. In terms of its architecture, it is a genius design from noted architect Mies van der Rohe, who was brought in by developer Herbert Greenwald in the late 1950s. Greenwald and other developers wanted to create "integrated communities" in hopes of attracting residents to a shrinking Detroit. After World War II, Detroit officials focused on "urban renewal" or a revitalization of some of the city's so-called declining neighborhoods.

As a result, the largely African American community known as Black Bottom was razed, eliminating African American homes and businesses in the process of creating a site for Lafayette Park. Van der Rohe's aesthetic and his ideas about how buildings should fit into their environment are clearly incorporated into the development with visible steel columns, floor-to-ceiling windows, and

## MIES VAN DER ROHE RESIDENTIAL DISTRICT

**WHAT** The residential area around Lafayette Park designed by famed architect Mies van der Rohe to replace Detroit's Black Bottom neighborhood.

**WHERE** Rivard St. at Lafayette Ave.

**COST** Free (private houses and not open to the public)

**PRO TIP** If someone offers you a private tour, take it. Otherwise, you'll have to rely on the rare real estate listing to get a glimpse of these stylish abodes.

*Architect Mies van der Rohe worked closely with landscape designers to balance his buildings with green areas, including a thirteen-acre green space known as The Plaisance.*

open floor plans throughout its apartments and townhouses. There are sizable park-like areas between the buildings thanks to landscape architect Alfred Caldwell, as well as recreational facilities and a school. Its roads and parking were built below grade so that you cannot see vehicles across the landscape. Although the development is close to downtown, it has a sense of calm that seems to pervade every home. Residents proudly follow van der Rohe's style through their furnishings—or lack thereof—in hopes of maintaining the architect's clean lines. The development, while economically stable throughout Detroit's turbulent decades, is a landmark now and its real estate is highly prized.

---

Lafayette Park is made up of three main housing types: High-rise apartments, townhouses, and courthouses.

# 52 KING OF THE BOOKS

**Where can you find every Detroit author from A to Z within the shelves of just one bookstore?**

If you can remember the title of your favorite childhood book or if you crave the complete works of a relatively unknown author, chances are the staff at John K. King Used & Rare Books can find these titles for you. John King is Michigan's largest used and rare bookstore.

What makes this fact even more amazing is that the store is completely uncomputerized—the people who work at John King simply know how everything is catalogued and where to find it. Well, some of its rare books are available for sale online, so the chain has grudgingly come into the digital age. King started small, selling his personal book collection at the Michigan Theatre, but quickly outgrew the quirky space. His current bookstore began in earnest in 1983 when he purchased what had been known up to that point as the Advance Glove Factory—that is why you can see a giant glove painted on the outside even to this day.

The four-story building had been abandoned and needed lots of love. Today, every nook and niche is filled with books from classic *Detroit Times* newspaper columnist Vera Brown to hard-boiled writer Elmore Leonard to Grosse Pointe novelist Jeffrey Eugenides. Every book is its own surprise; many have original photographs or newspaper clippings

---

Some of John King's rarest books include an original Mark Twain manuscript and a pamphlet written by John F. Kennedy when he was a Senator.

*John K. King Used & Rare Books is the city's classic bookstore, filled to the brim with novels, true crime, and every kind of literature in between.*

hidden inside. You never know what you'll find at John King books until you visit, so give yourself a couple of hours to browse the miles of shelves. You may even decide to sit down a spell and start reading.

## JOHN K. KING USED & RARE BOOKS

**WHAT** A four-story bookstore that features new, used, and rare books of every age and genre.

**WHERE** 901 W Lafayette Blvd.

**COST** Free but the books will cost you

**PRO TIP** It is said that John King has more than 1 million books in his total stock, so be nice to the staff there or you'll never find what you're looking for on the shelves.

**JAMES SCOTT MEMORIAL FOUNTAIN** (page 156)

**TINY HOUSE COMMUNITY** (page 20)

**VERTICAL EL CAMINO** (page 22)

***MAN IN THE CITY*** (page 24)

**1967 RIOT/REBELLION HISTORICAL MARKER** (page 40)

**THE TROWBRIDGE HOUSE** (page 42)

**CADIEUX CAFÉ** (page 48)

**ANNA SCRIPPS WHITCOMB CONSERVATORY** (page 84)

**THE BOY GOVERNOR** (page 60)

**MASONIC TEMPLE** (page 54)

**LIVINGSTONE MEMORIAL LIGHTHOUSE** (page 64)

**PSYCHEDELIC HEALING SHACK** (page 170)

**STE. ANNE DE DETROITS** (page 66)

ISAAC AGREE DOWNTOWN SYNAGOGUE (page 196)

**KERNS CLOCK** (page 94)

**C.A.N. ART HANDWORKS** (page 144)

MARINERS' CHURCH (page 68)

**MONUMENT TO JOE LOUIS** (page 178)

# 53 DETROIT'S BERLIN WALL

**Why would a housing developer purposely build a wall to isolate a Black neighborhood from a whites-only subdivision?**

Racially restrictive covenants—discriminatory practices that prevented African Americans from receiving low-interest loans and mortgages—were once standard practice in Detroit and across America. In fact, the federal government encouraged these racially motivated restrictions. One of the strangest abuses happened in Detroit when the Federal Housing Administration and the Home Owners' Loan Corporation refused to make loans to a developer for a housing project unless he built a six-foot high wall to separate his property from nearby homes owned by African Americans. The developer willingly erected the wall so he could receive the funding he wanted.

The Birwood Wall, which is only about one foot thick, goes for approximately a half mile south from Eight Mile Road to Pembroke Avenue and through the yards of houses along Birwood and Mendota streets. What remains of the Wall is now covered with murals, created by neighborhood residents and community activists in the early 2000s in hopes of turning something ugly into something meaningful. Yet no amount of paint can cover up what was

---

The Federal Housing Administration and the Home Owners' Loan Corporation created what is known as "redlining," or laws that denied loans and financial services to Black residents.

The Birwood Wall is also known as the Eight Mile Wall; it serves as a landmark of sorts reminding us all of local, state, and federal segregationist practices.

## EIGHT MILE WALL

**WHAT** A half-mile wall—with occasional breaks for roadways—built as a dividing line between the city's Black and white housing developments.

**WHERE** Birwood and Eight Mile Rds.

**COST** Free

**PRO TIP** Take the time to walk the entire wall so you can see the murals painted on it, including portraits of Rosa Parks and other heroic figures of the Black movement.

done in hate and with federal approval. Although these covenants and related laws were abolished, many African Americans still found higher-than-typical rents, housing restrictions, and related issues when buying homes in Detroit and many nearby communities through the 1970s.

# 54 HOT DOG HEAVEN

**How did two restaurant rivals that serve the same delicious dish end up next door to one another?**

Certain foods are synonymous with Detroit: Faygo pop, Better Made potato chips, and, of course, coney dogs.

A coney dog is a simple yet delicious link of protein: Take an all-meat, natural-casing hot dog, cover it with homemade chili sauce, sweet onions, and yellow mustard, and place it lovingly in a steamed bun. The coney dog is satisfying and delicious, making it a Detroit favorite for more than a century. But the debate over who makes the best Detroit coney dog has lasted for the same amount of time. Downtown, the debate centers on two restaurants: American Coney Island and Lafayette Coney Island. Their stories intertwine in a fascinating way. American, one of the oldest businesses in Detroit's downtown core, was founded

## AMERICAN CONEY ISLAND AND LAFAYETTE CONEY ISLAND

**WHAT** Two neighboring coney dog restaurants that were once operated by brothers Gust and William Keros.

**WHERE** 114 and 118 W Lafayette Ave.

**COST** Free to enter; coney dogs are about $2 each

**PRO TIP** Order fast, eat slow. And watch with awe as the restaurant staff stacks dozens of coneys on their arms to deliver to hungry patrons.

---

American Coney Island expanded its territory to include restaurants at Ford Field, the Detroit Zoo, and "The D" hotel in Las Vegas.

*The American-Lafayette debate over which restaurant serves the best coney dogs is as Detroit as music, automobiles, and sports.*

in 1917 by Constantine "Gust" Keros, who immigrated to Detroit from Greece in 1903. His business, selling coneys at a nickel each, was so successful that Keros encouraged his brother, William, to also come over from Greece. William learned the business from his sibling, took over the storefront next door and started Lafayette Coney Island. Lafayette uses its own recipes for the hot dog and its signature chili, setting up a rivalry that is legendary. If you are a "real" Detroiter, you identify with either American or Lafayette—it is practically illegal to stand neutral on this argument. Lafayette is owned by William's employees, who took it over upon his retirement. Gust's family still runs American, and his granddaughter Grace runs the restaurant like a military commander. Which coney is the best? That's up to each individual to decide.

# 55 UNDER THE SEA

**How did Detroit maintain the longest continuously running aquarium in the United States despite financial challenges?**

## BELLE ISLE AQUARIUM

**WHAT** The longest continuously operating aquarium and the only public aquarium in Michigan.

**WHERE** 900 Inselruhe Ave.

**COST** Free

**PRO TIP** Keep track of the Belle Isle Aquarium's calendar and you can help the volunteer move its beloved koi from their winter home inside the aquarium to its exterior pond.

When the Belle Isle Aquarium opened in 1904, it stood as a tribute to the city, its recreational investments, and the beauty that can only come from an Albert Kahn design. From the beginning, the aquarium was a special place for Detroiters to visit. Its sea-green glass, high dome, and seawater and freshwater tanks create a cool atmosphere that calms even the most savage beast.

Kahn designed the Beaux-Arts style facility to be perfect for strolling. A long hallway displays 44 tanks on both sides, giving every visitor a perfect view of the sea life within. Kahn wanted to make it seem like the fish were hanging like art pieces in an upscale gallery, so each tank is elevated

---

Despite stories to the contrary, Belle Isle Aquarium's stunning ceiling tiles are not Pewabic. They are rare green Opalite tiles meant to look like underwater glass.

*Fish, amphibians, and other sea life from across the globe are found within the Belle Isle Aquarium, a century-old facility beloved by Detroiters.*

to the viewer's eye level. The front of the brick building is just as glamorous as its interior with an ornate arch and detailed carvings of Neptune, the city's seal, and dolphins swimming alongside. Detroit's financial misfortunes caught up with its beloved aquarium in 2005, forcing officials to shutter the facility because of funding issues. The Belle Isle Conservancy reopened it in 2012, and a group of dedicated volunteers have kept it open. Since then, more than half a million people have gone through the aquarium, and its huge popularity continues to this day. Children of all ages continue to delight in seeing everything from gar to albino frogs to African lung fish—up close and personal.

# 56 MAKING MUSICAL HISTORY

**Everybody knows about Motown, but do you know about Detroit's other legendary music-recording studio?**

Miles Davis. Charlie Parker. John Lee Hooker. These musical talents all recorded some of their greatest work in Detroit at United Sound Systems Recording Studios. The business, established in 1933 inside what formerly served as a private residence, was the first independent and full-service major recording studio in the nation. It gave artists, writers, producers, and musicians a way to get their music recorded, in front of the public, and on the radio without needing a major record label.

Owner Jimmy Siracuse, an Italian immigrant, violinist, and recording engineer, created an atmosphere that attracted singers and jazz greats as well as other Detroit rockers such as the MC5, Bob Seger, and Isaac Hayes. Even Motown's founding father, Berry Gordy, recorded the first song he wrote at United Sound in 1959; it was a tune called "Come to Me" and sung by Marv Johnson. By the 1970s, United Sound was producing disco and funk—including George Clinton and Parliament Funkadelic—under the direction of its second owner, Don Davis. However, the studios fell under poor management, and a freeway project as well as a federal investigation threatened to shutter United Sound for good. A group of volunteers calling themselves the Detroit Sound

## UNITED SOUND

**WHAT** A music-recording studio where some rock, bebop, funk, and soul greats played over the decades.

**WHERE** 2648 W Grand Blvd.

**COST** Free

**PRO TIP** Take a studio tour and step up to the microphones that once amplified the tones of Annie Lennox and other greats.

*Artists from Aretha Franklin to the Doobie Brothers to Anita Baker have recorded some of their greatest hits inside United Sound.*

Conservancy re-energized the facility, brought new attention to its musical heritage, and began offering tours of the facility to an interested public. In 2017, United Sound received historic designation under the state of Michigan, bringing its legacy full circle.

---

Blues legend John Lee Hooker recorded the influential "Boogie Chillen'" single at United Sound in 1948. In an interview, Hooker said, "I wrote that song in Detroit when I was sittin' around strummin' my guitar. The thing come into me, you know?"

# 57 FACTORY MAN

**Where did Henry Ford, his engineers, and assembly workers put together his game-changing Model T?**

As the second home to Henry Ford's namesake automotive company, the Ford Piquette Avenue Plant is one of the most significant automotive heritage sites in the world. Ford chose the Milwaukee Junction neighborhood for his fledgling car company because of its proximity to two railroad lines (Detroit and Milwaukee), other auto companies, and suppliers. Ford's board spent $76,500 for its construction in April 1904. The three-story, Victorian-style brick building designed by architects Field, Hinchman & Smith was modeled after a textile mill. Employees assembled axles and engines on the first floor. Ford and his mechanics, engineers, and business managers had their offices on the second floor along with light machining and sub-assembly. The third floor had chassis assembly as well as the drafting and "experimental" rooms. The factory was considered state-of-the-art, and its most notable features are the 355 windows that gave its workers light and ventilation.

Ford and his staff, including business manager James Couzens, conceived of the Model T at the Piquette, and the first twelve thousand vehicles were assembled within its narrow walls. Ford Models including B, C, F, K, N, R, and S were also built at the Piquette. By 1907, Model N was the

---

The Piquette also has a large display of Dodge Brothers vehicles and materials as the two men supplied most of Ford's parts before starting their own company.

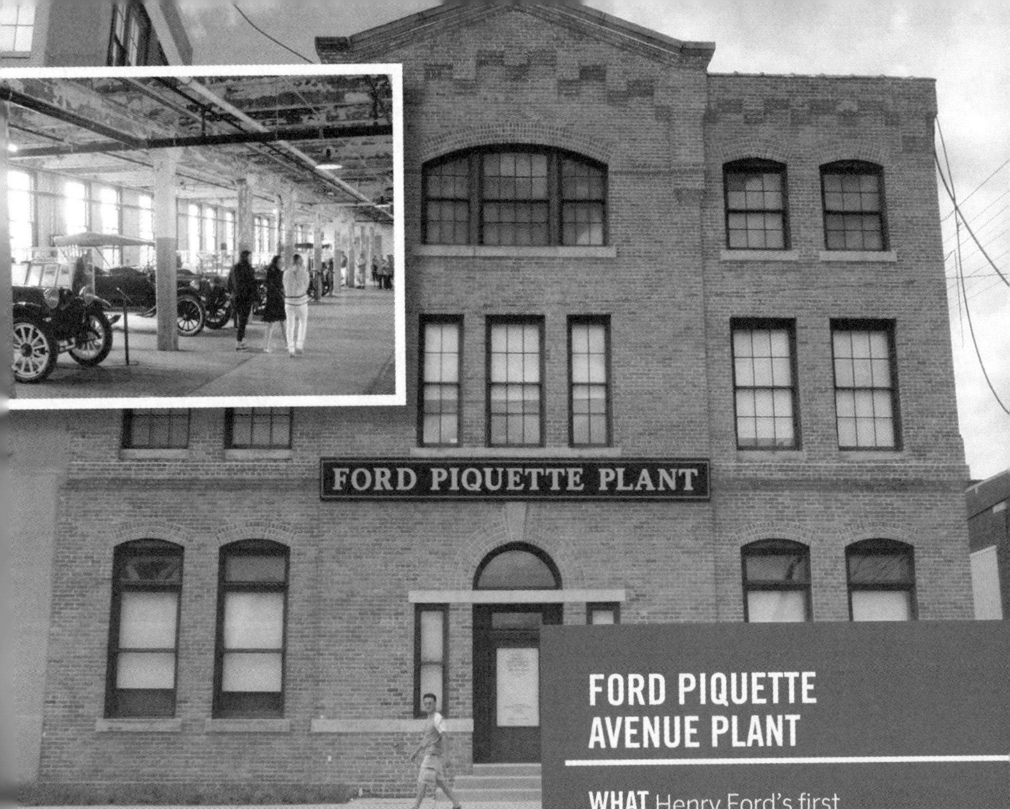


The Ford Piquette Avenue Plant has recreated Henry Ford's office, although he rarely spent time there. He preferred to be out on the floor.

## FORD PIQUETTE AVENUE PLANT

**WHAT** Henry Ford's first factory for the Model T and Model N, two of his most successful automotive designs.

**WHERE** 461 Piquette Ave.

**COST** $12 for adults to tour the facility

**PRO TIP** Take the factory tour with a docent if possible—most of these experts are former Ford employees or have vast automotive knowledge.

nation's best-selling car. As the company grew, the Piquette's size and space constraints were apparent. As a result, Ford moved production to the larger Highland Park Plant in 1910, selling the Piquette to Studebaker in 1911. Studebaker produced vehicles there until 1933. It housed a variety of companies from there, until the Model T Automotive Heritage Complex purchased it for use as a historic landmark in 2000. The Piquette is on the U.S. National Register of Historic Places and became a U.S. National Historic Landmark in 2006.

# 58 ONE WOMAN'S VOICE

**How did the words of a *Detroit News* columnist result in a fund-raising campaign and creation of a carillon?**

Before there was "Dear Abby" or Oprah Winfrey to help with life's problems, Detroiters had help through the widely read advice column of Nancy Brown. Brown was the pen name of Annie Louise (Brown) Leslie, a widow who became a journalist after her reporter husband passed away. When she moved to Michigan, Leslie showed up at *The Detroit News* and an editor brought her in to write women's stories. Leslie soon became the anonymous voice behind the newspaper's popular "Experience" column in 1919; shortly thereafter she started using the fake moniker of "Nancy Brown".

Her suggestions became gospel as Detroiters flocked to the events and places she recommended. In 1934, Brown wrote about her idea for a non-denominational religious service and asked readers to join her at sunrise on Belle Isle.

## NANCY BROWN PEACE CARILLON

**WHAT** A musical tower dedicated to the peaceful religious ceremonies suggested by *The Detroit News* columnist Nancy Brown, also known as Annie L. Leslie

**WHERE** Belle Isle

**COST** FREE

**PRO TIP** Annie Louise Brown's papers are available to the public at the Mount Holyoke College Library for further study.

The carillon's cornerstone reads:
"Dedicated to peace in honor of Nancy Brown by readers of her Experience Column in The Detroit News. A.D. 1939."

*Nancy Brown suggested the carillon tower be constructed on Belle Isle as a tribute to her readers and their peaceful connection to the island.*

An estimated thirty thousand people showed up that first time; attendance grew each subsequent year. One of her column readers suggested a monument to honor these first sunrise services, so Brown used her column to ask for donations to build a musical bell tower on Belle Isle. People willingly jumped on the assignment, sending in their nickels and dimes by the thousands. The tower, which cost about $59,000 to build, was designed by Clarence E. Day. The eighty-five-foot tower was dedicated at the seventh annual Sunrise Service in July 1940 in front of fifty thousand fans with Brown introducing herself to her readers for the first time. The tower's bronze doors have a portrait of Brown on them, writing away. Brown retired in 1942 and died in 1948, but her column continued with other writers at the *News* through 1985. To this day, the carillon's bells, now controlled by a computer, ring every half hour.

# 59 REVELATION POTTERY

**What pottery studio has an international reputation for "enriching the human spirit through clay?"**

Mary Chase Perry Stratton had an inventor's spirit. Much like Louis Comfort Tiffany and other artists at the turn of the 20th century, Stratton experimented with her artistic medium—in her case, ceramics. Her work with glazes changed the way people worked with this delicate artform, and more than a century later Stratton's technique is still lauded. Stratton had worked with clay from her childhood, and she proved so talented that she began private instruction in 1901 at the New York State School of Clay-Working. Around this time, Stratton formed several pivotal partnerships as she tried her ideas at firing and glazing with a small kiln. The result, according to one customer in 1903, were glazes that "are soft and dull, yet lustrous and of a texture that is a delight to the touch."

Her business grew so quickly that by 1906 she and her business partner, Horace Caulkins, open a new design studio on East Jefferson in 1907. Today, Pewabic tiles, vases, ornaments, and a variety of other decorative items are considered among the finest examples of Arts and Crafts pottery in the world. Most Metro Detroit homes have at least one example on a bookshelf or mantle, proving that people have appreciated the beauty of Stratton's iridescent glazes, colors, and exquisite patterns and have made them a part of their daily lives. Its facility has a retail store, classrooms, a studio, and a small museum where people of all ages learn about Stratton, her work as an educator, and Pewabic's unique design techniques.

*The Pewabic name, its iconic building, and its tiles stand for quality, and examples of Mary Chase Perry Stratton's work are found in homes across Metro Detroit.*

Pewabic is a Native American word for "metal" as well as the name of the copper mine in Stratton's hometown of Hancock, Michigan.

## PEWABIC POTTERY

**WHAT** An Arts and Crafts pottery studio that is known for its signature glazes, designs, and fabrication.

**WHERE** 10125 E Jefferson Ave.

**COST** Free to visit

**PRO TIP** You can make your own Pewabic tile through one of the many classes, day camps, and school field trips available through the non-profit organization that runs Pewabic.

# 60 FIREFIGHTERS' TRIBUTE

**What Detroit cemeteries have a special area designated just for deceased firefighters and one special little boy?**

Detroit has some of the nation's oldest cemeteries, and they serve as the resting places for the city's greatest politicians, business owners, and celebrities. But two locations—Mt. Elliott and Elmwood cemeteries—also have special places set aside just for firefighters. These areas, known as the Firemen's Lots, are spaces for the grave of any active or retired firefighter who is a member of what is known as the Fireman's Fund.

The Fireman's Fund is a century-old organization which paid benefits to the families of paid firemen who died on duty. Because it was expensive to bury firefighters individually, the Fund wanted each cemetery to designate one area for all. It originally purchased the large lots for $500 each in both Mt. Elliott and Elmwood in October 1872. Fund members already buried in each cemetery were

## THE FIREMEN'S LOTS

**WHAT** Specially designated burial lots set aside for active and retired firefighters in Mt. Elliott and Elmwood cemeteries.

**WHERE** 1200 Elmwood St.

**COST** Free to visit

**PRO TIP** Look for the statues of fire hydrants when you visit—that's one easy indicator that you're in the right spot to honor these heroes.

---

*Memorial Day services are held annually by the Detroit Firefighters Association. On even years, it is held in the Mt. Elliott plot and in odd years at Elmwood.*

*The Firemen's Lots at Elmwood and Mt. Elliott cemeteries both have statues and other monuments of firefighting equipment to designate these areas as special to this most noble profession.*

reinterred in the new Firemen's Lots. Why two cemeteries? That is because Mt. Elliott is a Catholic cemetery, and Elmwood is non-sectarian and, therefore, not restricted to a particular religious group. The Fireman's Fund also paid for monuments for both cemeteries to mark this special area; they were installed in 1889 and 1890. The Firefighter Lot is highlighted by a statue of a 19th century fireman atop a slim stone column. Beneath his stone feet are the words: "After life's turmoil peacefully sleep." Firemen of all ages and experience were included—with one exception. Mt. Elliott is the final resting place of a young boy named Gregory Thomas Andrews. Andrews wanted to be a fireman when he grew up, but he died at age five in 1977 of a malignant brain tumor. When firemen next door to the cemetery heard about him, they lined up their firetrucks around the fence in his honor and flashed their lights. He is buried next to his heroes for all time.

# 61 A FOREST IN THE CITY

**How did one of Detroit's oldest cemeteries earn a respected title as an arboretum?**

Detroit is the home of many famous "firsts." But what might surprise you is that one of the city's most revered burial grounds became its first certified arboretum as well. In 2015, Elmwood Cemetery received this special accreditation for its standards and professional practices from the ArbNet and the Morton Register of Arboreta, a group that has a database of the locations of tree-focused public gardens around the world. According to ArbNet, an arboretum is a specialized type of botanical garden that focuses on trees and other woody plants. Arboreta collect, grow, and display trees, shrubs, and other plants for people to study and enjoy. During the certification process, Elmwood officials surveyed all of its trees and tagged them, creating a record of species as well as the location and condition of each tree.

Among its 1,450 recorded trees, there are ninety-one species within the cemetery's eighty-six acres including ash, beech, willow, hawthorn, and American plum. These trees and all of the greenery were very much part of the overall plan for the venerable cemetery, which began in 1846

### ELMWOOD CEMETERY NAMED DETROIT'S FIRST CERTIFIED ARBORETUM

**WHAT** Through the vision of noted landscape architect Frederick Law Olmsted, Detroit's Elmwood Cemetery and its many trees earned recognition from ArbNet and the Morton Register of Arboreta.

**WHERE** 1200 Elmwood St.

**COST** Free

**PRO TIP** Elmwood offers regular tours of its certified arboretum, giving visitors a look at the many trees, plants, and flowers on the grounds.

*Elmwood Cemetery is the oldest, non-denominational, continuously operating cemetery in Michigan. It also is Detroit's first certified arboretum.*

with forty-two acres of farmland. Prominent landscape architect Frederick Law Olmsted in 1890 designed Elmwood to create "park-like grounds, graceful hills, and a calmly flowing stream" through the original property. Olmsted, who also designed New York City's beloved Central Park, hoped to recreate the look of Mount Auburn in Cambridge, Massachusetts, as part of his overall design for Elmwood. He also advised Elmwood's caretakers to focus on native trees as well as careful pruning and overall land management. Thanks to his unique vision, Elmwood has large stands of trees as well as gently sloping roads that follow the natural shape of the property.

---

When it received its certification, an Elmwood Cemetery spokesperson said that there are plans to add more than four hundred additional trees to its property over the next decade.

# 62 FARM FRESH

**What is the largest historic public market district in the United States?**

Known affectionately to locals as "The Sheds," these hulking open-air markets are places where you can find everything from fresh milk to fresh flowers to the best food trucks in the city. They all co-exist peacefully under the roof of Detroit's beloved Eastern Market. Around 1891, farms began gathering at a central location along Gratiot Road about a mile northeast of downtown, selling their wares to eager customers. With its ramshackle sheds, Eastern Market became Detroit's center for the wholesale and retail trade of food products. By World War II, Eastern Market covered forty-three acres with the center being a six-block public market and another eighty storefronts nearby. This array of business and commercial facilities surrounds the main marketplace sheds, all serving to create a lively location to buy and sell goods. Its annual events, especially Flower Day, have made Eastern Market the largest open-air flowerbed market in the United States.

Today, thanks to contributions to the non-profit organization that runs Eastern Market and its own funds, Eastern Markets sheds are in top shape and busier than ever. Eastern Market is a business incubator, gathering space, and regular public market that serves the community fresh food, produce, spices, jams and much more. As fast as

---

Eastern Market is open year-round, and during the busy summer months it attracts as many as fifty thousand visitors a week.

*The various food and beverage vendors on site most Tuesdays and Sundays at Eastern Market have fed Detroiters for generations.*

Eastern Market has grown, the appetite for its friendly service, unique offerings, and devotion to the public good has grown right along with it. The Eastern Market Historic District was added to the National Registry of Historic Places in 1978.

## EASTERN MARKET HISTORIC DISTRICT

**WHAT** A largely open-air marketplace with sheds, neighboring two-story Victorian business fronts, and restaurants devoted to fine food, fine dining, and the development of new food businesses.

**WHERE** 2934 Russell St.

**COST** Free/pay as you shop

**PRO TIP** Come hungry and bring something to carry all of the goods, flowers, and food you are likely to buy when you're on-site.

# 63 METAL CRAFT

**Why are there windmills, red stick figures shooting arrows, and other metal sculptures peeking out from a corner near Eastern Market?**

Carl A. Nielbock started his career as a blacksmith, using extreme heat to bend metal to his will. Born in Celle, Germany, the artist-in-training studied the European masters, especially its architects, for inspiration. Nielbock moved to Detroit in 1984 and started his own workshop on the city's East side, just outside of the Eastern Market district.

Today, through his high-profile work at C.A.N. Art Handworks Inc., Nielbock crafts metal into all shapes and sizes in a way that pleases the eyes and mind. He not only creates landmarks, he serves as the main repairman for many of the city's icons, including the Fox Theatre, the Spirit of Detroit statue, the Hurlbut Memorial Gate, and Gateway to Freedom International Memorial. His work honors his past in postwar Germany but also has a decidedly forward focus. His workspace is a three-floor artist's haven, filled with his art, architectural ornaments, and metal sculptures. Partly inspired by Tyree Guyton's Heidelberg Project, Nielbock displays many pieces of his visionary work on his small campus outside so people can see them. Visitors will find examples of his exquisite gates, red stick figures

---

Carl Nielbock restored the Fort Wayne cannons using old military manuals; in return, he can use its 1800s-era blacksmith shop.

*Through his C.A.N. Art Handworks business, Carl Nielbock is working on some of Detroit's oldest and newest metal projects, including a restoration of its old city hall clock.*

commemorating Detroit's part in the Battle of Bloody Run, windmills, and the often-photographed "Detroit" sign along the fence. C.A.N. Art is especially notable for its "sky garden," a three-story deck supported by four salvaged Detroit light poles.

## C.A.N. ART HANDWORKS

**WHAT** An art studio and sculpture park known for its elaborate metal work and inspiring pieces.

**WHERE** 2264 Wilkins St.

**COST** Free (unless you commission a piece)

**PRO TIP** Nielbock opens his studio to the public for special events, so keep an eye out for times and dates. Otherwise, this is a private business so be respectful when you visit.

# 64 FOUND ART

**Why is there a large sculpture garden with huge metal art objects located near a busy freeway in Detroit?**

They stand like metal soldiers, each one solitary on its simple base. They are the master works of local artist Robert Sestok, who took a small plot of Detroit land and turned it into City Sculpture art park. Sestok, who considers Detroit and the Cass Corridor area as his main inspirations, created the non-profit park as a way to bring experimental sculpture work to the public eye.

Sestok's goal in part was to create a rotating exhibition schedule showing the works of many visiting artists to keep the park interesting—not only for him but for the general public. Sestok works in a variety of mediums: Metal through his welding shop, printmaking, and painting in a Detroit-based studio. As a native Detroiter, Sestok followed the developments and

### CITY SCULPTURE

**WHAT** An art park displaying the large-scale and experimental sculpture work of longtime Cass Corridor artist Robert Sestok.

**WHERE** 955 W Alexandrine St.

**COST** Free

**PRO TIP** Look for Sestok's use of bronze welded steel and stainless steel in his works, which are found both in the City Sculpture park as well as around the city.

Eventually, founder Robert Sestok wants City Sculpture to be a site for classes and workshops in sculptural art with visiting artists giving lectures and demonstrations.

*About a dozen sculptures are on display at City Sculpture art park, and there is room for many more as Sestok and his friends complete them.*

reorganization of the city in his art, looking for found objects, non-traditional materials, and processes that documented the way Detroit was always in the midst of reconstruction. For his sculptures, Sestok shifts between what he calls positive cuts, such as a silhouette representing man, to negative cuts which express architecture or environmental space. Welding helps him create permanency and sculptures that can withstand the elements, like those on display at City Sculpture for locals, visitors, Wayne State University students, and young people from nearby public schools.

# 65 STRIKE A POSE

**Why is there a giant bowling pin in the parking lot of a Detroit taqueria?**

Southwest Detroit is one of the city's most diverse areas, but it may be best known for its strong Hispanic population. A popular attraction for visitors and residents alike are the Mexican bakeries, restaurants, and supermarkets that dot the neighborhood.

One landmark eatery has arguably the best tacos in town, but also one of the most memorable attractions. A large white three-dimensional bowling pin sits in the Mi Pueblo parking lot, a welcoming sight as you drive up to this local mainstay. If you pull into the lot, look for it leaning up against a tall tree sandwiched between parking spaces. It's a local favorite for taking pictures, especially for teens who want to post a selfie of themselves with the bowling pin on social media.

No one really knows where the bowling pin came from or how it ended up at one of the tastiest Mexican eateries

## GIANT-SIZED BOWLING PIN

**WHAT** A 10-foot tall bowling pin serves as a landmark in the Mi Pueblo parking lot.

**WHERE** 7278 Dix St.

**COST** Free

**PRO TIP** Make sure to go inside the restaurant for a Mexican feast.

---

*Mi Pueblo patterns its food and drink after the owners' hometown of Jalisco, Mexico, serving tacos, tortas, enchiladas, and salsa roja by the gallon.*

*It is a bit scuffed up from its travels, but the Mi Pueblo bowling pin is an ideal backdrop for social-media snaps, family pictures, or bowling team photos.*

in the city. Granted, Detroit has one of the largest numbers of registered bowlers in the nation, so perhaps that is why it draws a regular crowd. Perhaps a defunct bowling alley needed a home for its woebegone attraction. Whatever the reason, the giant bowling pin is a beacon for people of all ages, inspiring many to visit and stay a while for a warm meal, a cool soda, and maybe even a Margarita.

# 66 CODE NAME "MIDNIGHT"

**Why was Detroit a significant stop on the Underground Railroad and what landmarks remain?**

The life-saving network known as the Underground Railroad had one of its final U.S. stops in Detroit, and the city has embraced its history through a variety of tours, exhibits, and landmarks. According to the Detroit Historical Society, Michigan had at least seven known paths that led slaves to freedom to Canada, and there were an estimated two hundred Underground Railroad stops in the state from 1820 to 1865. Two places of note are Second Baptist Church and the Path to Freedom sculpture.

Second Baptist Church was founded by freed slaves and is the oldest religious institution owned by Blacks in the Midwest. It also served as a station on the Underground Railroad for three decades, working with abolitionist leaders including Sojourner Truth and Frederick Douglass. Its basement safe house, known as the Croghan Street Station, is one of the last documented Detroit stations left today. Second Baptist Church is said to have moved an estimated five thousand slaves from Detroit to Canada, giving them food, clothing, and shelter as part of its mission to free slaves and provide

## DETROIT'S PART IN THE UNDERGROUND RAILROAD

**WHAT** Detroit has a variety of tours, events, and landmarks to honor its role in the Underground Railroad.

**WHERE** Second Baptist Church, 441 Monroe Ave., Hart Plaza

**COST** Free; church tours are available for a small fee

**PRO TIP** For a comprehensive tour, check out Black Scroll Network History and Tours, which offers African American-themed tours with an emphasis on Detroit's Black history.

*The* Gateway to Freedom *sculpture is placed along the Detroit River in Hart Plaza to symbolize the path people took to escape from slavery to Windsor or other parts of Canada.*

them with "the full privileges of American citizenship," church officials said. Another must-see is the *Gateway to Freedom* International Memorial, a sculpture in Hart Plaza along the Detroit RiverWalk. The sculpture shows Underground Railroad conductor and Detroit resident George DeBaptiste and a group of slaves preparing to cross the Detroit River. According to its creator, African American sculptor Ed Dwight, the *Gateway to Freedom* features two gateway pillars that bracket a ten-foot by twelve-foot sculpture with nine slaves and a railroad 'Conductor' looking and pointing toward Canada in anticipation of boarding the boat across the Detroit River to safety. A companion statue, also by Dwight, is across the river in Windsor.

---

Museums such as the Detroit Historical Museum and Charles H. Wright Museum of African American History and several churches including the Historic First Congregational Church of Detroit have Underground Railroad tours and exhibits.

# 67 A TRIBUTE TO MANUFACTURING

**What group of murals in the Detroit Institute of Arts inspired so much controversy that thousands of people signed petitions to have them removed?**

The Detroit Institute of Arts had four blank walls inside a centrally located courtyard, and museum patron Edsel Ford wanted to see them filled with a mural inspired by Detroit history and industrial development. Ford and DIA Director William Valentiner went to one of the most dynamic and outspoken painters of the day in hopes that he would take on the job.

Mexican muralist Diego Rivera arrived in Detroit and explored the Ford manufacturing plant along the Rouge River. Rivera had agreed to paint two murals, but he was so inspired by what he saw that he suggested doing four murals in all. Art critics agree the result is one of the most dramatic and valuable murals not only in the United States but in all of North America. Rivera started painting in July 1932, creating sprawling murals of the Ford assembly line of the 1932 Ford V-8 and Detroit's chemical, medical, and pharmaceutical industries, as well as cultural icons depicting fertility and creation. From the moment the murals were

---

Frida Kahlo, Rivera's spouse and muse, accompanied him to Detroit. The trip, which became tragic when she lost a pregnancy, still proved inspirational for the young artist.

*Diego Rivera considered the DIA murals to be the best work of his career, and art critics call it the finest example of Mexican mural art in the United States.*

unveiled in 1933, they sparked controversy and, in some cases, disdain. A *Detroit News* editorial described Rivera's work as "coarse," "foolishly vulgar," and "a slander to Detroit workmen." Ford defended the murals, ignoring calls to destroy or whitewash them. Today, Rivera's work is regarded as a vibrant reminder of the city's past, its longtime commitment to the auto industry, and the struggles of labor, sentiments the famous Marxist had probably hoped to engender. The murals are so beloved within the city that the site is in high demand as a wedding location—a tribute to Rivera, his wife Frida Kahlo, and the museum itself for its bold commission of a then-controversial artist.

## DETROIT INDUSTRY FRESCO CYCLE

**WHAT** A 27-panel work of art that highlight's Detroit's manufacturing base and labor force during the pivotal 1930s.

**WHERE** 5200 Woodward Ave.

**COST** Free if you're a resident of Wayne, Oakland, or Macomb counties

**PRO TIP** If you study the panels, you can find many Detroit luminaries within the murals, including Henry Ford himself standing next to a car engine that operates with the legs of a dog.

# 68 REDLINING REBELLION

**How did the purchase of a home in Detroit pit neighbor against neighbor in a landmark U.S. Supreme Court case?**

Orsel and Minnie McGhee were like any family—they were renting a home in Detroit they enjoyed, so they decided to purchase it and live the American Dream. Only their dream turned into a nightmare when their purchase sparked abuse, threats, and worse. The house on Seebaldt was under a neighborhood association agreement, which included a covenant restricting its occupancy to "whites only."

The McGhees, who were African American, refused to move from their longtime home. Two courts, including the Michigan Supreme Court, agreed with the local covenant. The case came before the U.S. Supreme Court in 1948, and the court combined it with a similar case from St. Louis (Shelley v. Kramer) in hopes of settling the matter once and for all. The McGhees were represented by NAACP's attorney Thurgood Marshall, who would become a Supreme Court justice himself. The nation's highest court ruled that any covenant restricting residence on the basis of race was unconstitutional because of the

## ORSEL AND MINNIE MCGHEE HOUSE

**WHAT** The home of an African American couple whose 1944 purchase of a home on Detroit's near west side resulted in the U.S. Supreme Court affirming the protections of the Fourteenth Amendment.

**WHERE** 4626 Seebaldt St.

**COST** Free

**PRO TIP** The historical marker outside the McGhee house is located next to what remains a private residence; consider the homeowners' privacy when viewing it or taking pictures.

*The McGhee House was one of two cases used to break down racial covenants that prevented African Americans from purchasing homes in largely white neighborhoods.*

Fourteenth Amendment. That Amendment, passed after the Civil War, prohibits the states from denying "to any person ... the equal protection of the law." According to the State Bar of Michigan, "Orsel and Minnie McGhee had secured not only their home, but the rights of all to buy homes free of restrictive racial covenants."

---

**While the court cases were largely considered a victory, real estate developers in and around Detroit continued to use racial covenants well into the 1960s and 1970s.**

# 69 ODE TO A SCOUNDREL

**What beloved landmark was created to appease the will of one of Detroit's least-popular businessmen?**

Money has its way of making things happen, and James Scott knew that fact very well. The real estate speculator and developer was a Detroit legend in his own time, earning a reputation for his quick temper, poor public behavior, and tendency to sue his supposed enemies.

When Scott died in 1910, he donated his estate to the city to build a monument for residents. But there was one caveat: Scott also demanded that a statue be built in his honor. That is how the James Scott Memorial Fountain and neighboring sculpture of Scott seated in a grand chair came to be on the western end of Belle Isle. To build it, Detroit brought in two hundred acres of fill from downtown to expand Belle Isle for the ideal site. Cass Gilbert designed the fountain, and Herbert Adams had the job of creating the accompanying

## JAMES SCOTT MEMORIAL FOUNTAIN

**WHAT** An elaborate water fountain dedicated to the people of Detroit from one of the city's most infamous scoundrels.

**WHERE** Sunset Dr., Belle Isle

**COST** Free

**PRO TIP** Wait until after dark to visit Belle Isle so you can see the fountain lit up at night for a grand display.

---

*Detroit lore has it that James Scott irritated people so much that his statue was placed in a way that allows the fountain's spray to hit him in the face.*

*The chair where Scott sits has a dedication on it that some old-time Detroiters may find ironic: "From the good deed of one comes benefit to many."*

sculpture of James Scott. Gilbert, who also designed the Detroit Public Library, created a masterful monument—the fountain is 510 feet in circumference with Vermont white marble bowls topped with a receptacle that projects water forty feet into the air. It is decorated with 109 water outlets in the shapes of lions, turtles, and Neptune figures as well as sixteen bas-relief panels depicting early Detroit life. The basin originally had Pewabic tiles on it, but vandalism and other damage destroyed them by the early 2000s. Adams created his Scott sculpture out of bronze and placed it on a marble pedestal overlooking the fountain and facing the city. While Scott's character might have been suspect, his gift to the city is likely the best thing Scott ever did.

# 70 PAPAL BLESSINGS

**Where else would a Polish Pope visit than one of the most Polish cities in America?**

Let's just say Karol Józef Wojtyla is a rock star in Hamtramck. There are statues of him, tributes dedicated in his name, and a permanent display of his clothing. Better known as Pope John Paul II, his September 1987 trip to Hamtramck was like a religious holiday. Residents, city officials, and religious representatives went all out when Pope John Paul II came for his first Papal visit. Pope John Paul II arrived at Metro Airport and took a helicopter ride into Detroit to visit Sacred Heart Major Seminary.

His first stop the next morning was Hamtramck, where the large Polish population turned out in droves to see their native son. The Pope took part in a parade and celebration before heading to Hart Plaza for another speech. He then went to the Pontiac Silverdome, where the cheering for the Catholic religious leader rivaled that of a championship football game. Nearly 100,000 attended the Pope's celebration of Mass, which many said was one of the most moving religious ceremonies of their lives.

St. Florian Church still has the vestments Pope John Paul II wore during that Silverdome mass on permanent display in a small room off its main entrance. Hamtramck also boasts two other Pope John Paul II memorials—one commemorating his 1987 visit and a statue in Pope John Paul II Park at the corner of Joseph Campau and Belmont Streets that commemorates his visit to Hamtramck in September 1969, before he became Pope.

*Icons of Pope John Paul II—who was born in Wadowice, Poland—are found throughout Hamtramck, a small city within Detroit whose population was once half Polish.*

Pope John Paul II visited Hamtramck multiple times, including a 1969 visit when he was the cardinal archbishop of Krakow.

## A POPE'S VESTMENTS

**WHAT** The vestments from when Pope John Paul II celebrated Mass at the Pontiac Silverdome along with photographs from his visit.

**WHERE** 2626 Poland St., Hamtramck

**COST** Free

**PRO TIP** St. Florian also hosts an annual firefighters' mass on the first Saturday in May in conjunction with its popular Strawberry Festival.

# 71 A PRICELESS COLLECTION

## Whose portrait is one of the most valuable pieces inside the Detroit Institute of Arts?

Vincent van Gogh is known for his dramatic paintings and equally dramatic life. Although he lived only a short time, van Gogh's artwork is appreciated throughout the world.

The Detroit Institute of Arts acquired his *Self Portrait with a Straw Hat* in 1922, making it the first van Gogh painting to enter a U.S. museum collection. This self-portrait—one of many he painted—was created in 1877. It shows the artist in profile with a jaunty straw hat on his red hair. Van Gogh looks at the viewer with wide eyes and a bemused look on his pale face. Art experts estimated that the van Gogh self-portrait alone is worth as much as $150 million. Another DIA acquisition, van Gogh's *Portrait of the Postman Joseph Roulin* from 1888, is worth between $80 to $120 million. In all, the DIA has more than one

### *SELF PORTRAIT WITH A STRAW HAT*

**WHAT** The first Vincent van Gogh painting to enter a U.S. museum collection.

**WHERE** 5200 Woodward Ave.

**COST** Priceless (but free to see if you live within the three counties around the museum)

**PRO TIP** Plan to spend the day—there is so much to see and do at the Museum as well as a great spot to stop and chat, like the Kresge Court.

---

The Detroit Institute of Arts has five Vincent van Gogh paintings in its world-class collection.

*Vincent van Gogh painted around twenty self-portraits around the time that he created the one that now hangs in the Detroit Institute of Arts.*

hundred galleries with more than sixty-five thousand works. It is considered among the top six collections in the United States with a value of more than $1 billion. Although the DIA collection is one of the city's greatest assets, officials during the 2013 Detroit bankruptcy thought about selling some of these artworks. Using the art as a way to offset the city's debts and shore up its pensions was considered reasonable in a legal sense. However, public outcry by residents, foundations, and business leaders was so strong that the city did not act on this idea. Instead, an agreement called the "Grand Bargain" ensured there were enough funds to cover the city's pension funds during the reorganization. The DIA was allowed to become an independent institution apart from the city during this time, ensuring its art will be forever protected.

# 72 HAIL TO THE DETROITERS

**What university now known for its Ann Arbor location was actually founded in Detroit?**

Most people know the University of Michigan for its sprawling campus, a place where Maize and Blue dominate the landscape. But the prestigious learning institution actually began in downtown Detroit, not in leafy Ann Arbor. The story begins on August 26, 1817, when Lewis Cass—the governor of the Michigan territory—and territory judges including Reverend John Monteith, Fr. Gabriel Richard, and Judge Augustus Woodward enacted a bill that established the University of Michigania. Its single building was located on Bates Street near Cadillac Square.

Granted, Detroit only had about twelve hundred people at the time, but they wanted a real school. The university was reorganized in 1821, but a lack of funding resulted in the governing board selling its land and renting out the Bates building to private schoolmasters. On March 18, 1837, a plan created by John Davis Pierce was approved by the state legislature and the new University of Michigan while a Board of Regents was established. Ann Arbor land developers gave the fledgling institution forty acres of land as a birthday gift of sorts, and that land is what

### THE FOUNDING OF THE UNIVERSITY OF MICHIGANIA

**WHAT** A plaque noting the 1817 founding of the state's largest public university in Detroit.

**WHERE** Behind 500 Woodward Ave. on Congress St.

**COST** Free

**PRO TIP** Impress your friends by describing the university as a "Catholepistemiad," a word Augustus Woodward created to mean a "system of universal science."

*In September 2017, the University of Michigan put a giant Wolverine jersey on the Spirit of Detroit in honor of its bicentennial. Photo courtesy of Roger Hart.*

is affectionately now known to students as the Diag. In 2001, officials mounted a Michigan Historical Marker on the wall of a parking structure near the intersection of Bates and Congress to note the university's founding in Detroit. The original U of M building had been dismantled in 1858, and the parking structure adjacent to the Comerica Tower was closest to the original site.

---

U of M is said to be modeled on the University of France, created by Napoléon Bonaparte in 1807, as "the center of a statewide system of primary, secondary, and college education."

# 73 THE DOORKEEPER

**Why is the casket of a Capuchin monk named Bernard Francis (Solanus) Casey on display at the St. Bonaventure Monastery?**

In 1958, the Capuchin Minister General called Fr. Solanus Casey "an extraordinary example of a true Capuchin and a replica of St. Francis." The quiet Capuchin was well known during his lifetime as a holy man of God and for his mantra of "Let us thank God ahead of time." The public got to know Fr. Solanus as porter of the door at St. Bonaventure Monastery, where he met people of every kind and at all hours. There, his welcoming nature earned him the nickname of "The Doorman." People began to seek his counsel when word of physical and spiritual healings were credited to his prayers and intercessions.

Fr. Solanus also is beloved in Detroit for helping to establish the Capuchin Soup Kitchen in 1929 during the Great Depression, which hit Detroit and its automobile industry harder than most places. Upon his death in July 1957, Fr. Solanus's remains were moved from the friars' cemetery and into the north transept of the St. Bonaventure Monastery chapel. The casket where he is interred is now part of the Solanus Casey Center, where thousands have viewed him, prayed over and for him and asked for his intercession on their behalf. In 1995, Pope John Paul II declared Fr. Solanus "Venerable" and described his life as one of "heroic virtue." In November 2017, Fr. Solanus received Beatification under Pope Francis and the title of "Blessed." His casket was again exhumed to obtain relics as part of this ceremony and he was reinterred in a new casket. It is hoped that if the Vatican approves another Solanus miracle he could advance to sainthood.

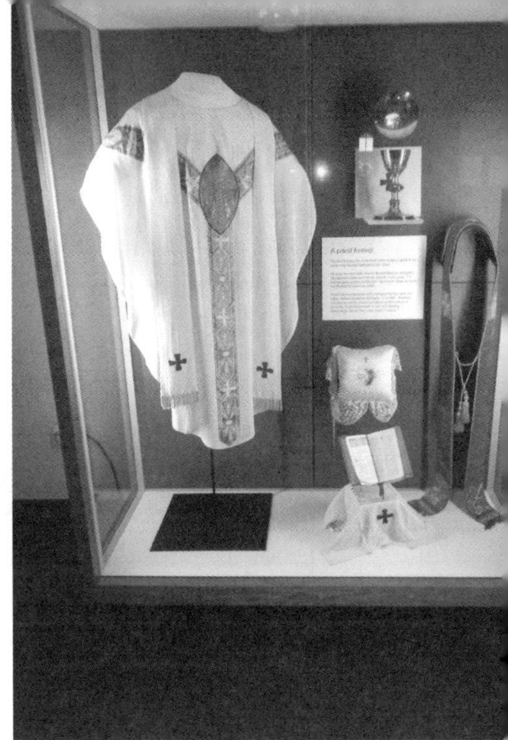

*Visitors from around the world visit and pray before the casket of Fr. Solanus Casey at a special center dedicated in his name on Detroit's East side.*

Fr. Solanus Casey was born near Milwaukee on November 25, 1870, the sixth of sixteen children, to Irish immigrants Bernard James Casey and Ellen Elizabeth (née Murphy) Casey.

## SOLANUS CASEY CENTER

**WHAT** The Tomb of Solanus Casey

**WHERE** 1780 Mount Elliott St.

**COST** Free but donations accepted

**PRO TIP** If you leave a note with a special intention on top of the casket, the monks will pray on behalf of your request.

# 74 THIRD FORT'S THE CHARM

**What military facility has stood guard over the city and yet has never seen any combat?**

Around 1840, U.S. military officials began looking around the vast farmlands near the Detroit River for a good spot to establish a new artillery post. They found the ideal piece of land at the river's bend and constructed a five-point star fort.

The complex, which was state-of-the-art for the mid-1800s, was named after General Anthony Wayne, who defeated the British in 1796 to help the United States acquire the Northwest Territories. The U.S. Army used the fort from 1841 to 1972, yet it has never had a shot fired in combat because of the nation's longtime and friendly relationships with England and Canada. Instead, it has been used throughout its history as an induction center for Michigan's men and women who served in American military conflicts from the Civil War to Vietnam. The fort had short terms of housing Italian prisoners of war during World War II and some Detroit families displaced by the violence after the 1967 riots/rebellions. Although the fort is in some disrepair, it has a devoted volunteer crew through the Historic Fort Wayne Coalition. They hold regular tours

---

Fort Wayne was the third fort built in Detroit—the first was France's Fort Pontchartrain du Détroit located near modern Hart Plaza, and the second was the Brits' Fort Lernoult, at the intersection of Fort and Shelby Streets.

Tours include Fort Wayne's original 1848 limestone barracks building, 1845 fort (renovated in 1861), the restored Commanding Officers house, the Spanish-American War guard house, and a Native American burial mound.

## FORT WAYNE

**WHAT** TAn 1841 fort that served as an induction center for military personnel.

**WHERE** 6325 W Jefferson Ave.

**COST** $5 for tours

**PRO TIP** Fort Wayne opens to the public on regular occasions for reenactments, historically accurate baseball games, and tours.

for visitors, and the Coalition's Civil War reenactments are among its most memorable events because they include actors portraying President Abraham Lincoln and other dignitaries. The Fort also is home to a Native American burial mound, which is now protected, having been through several earlier excavations.

# 75 A CITY WITHIN THE CITY

**What Detroit building is so large that it earned its own zip code?**

It has been called the flashiest piece of real estate in Detroit, and it is large enough to command its own zip code: 48243.

### THE RENAISSANCE CENTER

**WHAT** A five-building complex that serves as office space for General Motors Corporation and dozens of other companies.

**WHERE** 100 Renaissance Center

**COST** Free to visit

**PRO TIP** Download the Renaissance Center app before you visit. Although it is easier to get around after GM's renovation, you can still get lost easily.

The Renaissance Center is a city within a city, housing more than 10,000 daily employees, a 1,400-room hotel, and dozens of restaurants within its five towers. Altogether, the complex has more than 2.2 million square feet of space to work in and wander. Known among Detroiters as the Ren Cen, the office complex was the brainchild of Henry Ford II and other civic leaders, hoping to boost development within Detroit after the 1967 riot/rebellion. Construction began in 1973 and it was completed on July 1, 1976. At the time it opened, Ren Cen was the tallest hotel in the world. However, detractors have said its design was equivalent to

---

Since General Motors Corporation became the owner and main occupant of the facility, the building has been rebranded the GMRENCEN.

*The Renaissance Center dominates Detroit's skyline with its massive towers.*

its shape, which from the right angle looks like a hand sticking up the middle finger.

The seventy-three-story building does dominate the Detroit skyline, and its design and use remained controversial for decades. Over those years, the Ren Cen has housed a variety of tenants, including Ford Motor Company. In 1996, General Motors Corporation bought the facility to serve as its headquarters. The GM renovations, which topped $500 million, have made the building easier to navigate. GM also added the beautiful five-story glass atrium known as Wintergarden, which has outstanding views of the Detroit River and is a great spot to eat lunch purchased from the nearby food court. You also cannot beat the view from the higher floors, where there are several upscale restaurants.

# 76 WHERE IT'S AT

**Where in Detroit can you grab an organic juice, a massage, and a chiropractic adjustment and end up with a "whole outlook of positiveness?"**

Leave your inhibitions at the door when you walk into what is known in Detroit as the Psychedelic Healing Shack. What started as a chiropractic office has grown into a kind of commune for people looking for healing, vegetarian food, and an uplifting community spirit. On the exterior, the Healing Shack is painted a bright sunshine-yellow punctuated with a rainbow of vines, flowers, honeycombs, and other all-natural images.

There's a bonfire pit, a two-story treehouse for impromptu gatherings, and regular drum circles. Inside, several businesses coexist in peaceful harmony, including the Goldengate Café, an organic and vegetarian-friendly eatery. There also are a variety of

## PSYCHEDELIC HEALING SHACK

**WHAT** A "healing center" that combines a café with a holistic chiropractic practice.

**WHERE** 18700 Woodward Ave.

**COST** Free to visit; each retailer has his or her own prices

**PRO TIP** Keep track of the shack's event schedule as it regularly hosts musical, artistic, community, and cultural events along with its Wednesday night drum circles.

---

*Dr. Bob Pizzimenti is known for his unique style of energy healing, looking at the patient as water or "chi."*

*The Psychedelic Healing Shack's bright and cheerful exterior is what makes it so easy to find along Woodward Avenue.*

individual entrepreneurs selling everything from essential oils to healing crystals to medicinal herbs. Then there are the holistic chiropractic practices of Dr. Robert Pizzimenti, the Healing Shack's founder and community organizer. "Dr. Bob," as he is known to everyone who works at or visits the Psychedelic Healing Shack, purchased the building at the corner of Woodward and Goldengate near Seven Mile in the summer of 2000, hoping to create a healing center for the masses and new connections in an otherwise struggling set of neighborhoods. As a result of his open and welcoming nature, Dr. Bob has people of all ages, lifestyles, and spiritual backgrounds gathering at the Healing Shack, adding a groovy touch of good will to Detroit.

# 77 GREAT GLASS

**Where in Detroit can you find examples of religious and residential art created by the famed Tiffany Studios?**

There are no words to accurately describe the moment when sunlight comes streaming through a Tiffany stained glass window—you simply stand back in awe and wonder. Louis Comfort Tiffany began his career as a painter, and the combination of his sharp eye and deft hand is clear in all of his works, especially those found within the city of Detroit.

There are several examples of Tiffany Studios's work in the city, and it could be argued that they are some of the finest in the world. For example, there is the Beecher Mansion on the Wayne State University campus. From the exterior, the window is beautiful with subtle colors and intricate shapes. But from the inside, the exquisite nature of the windows comes to life with vibrant and saturated colors. And when the light hits just right, you feel like you are seeing a little vision of heaven.

Another stunning example is at Christ Church Detroit, an Episcopal church with a stained-glass portrait of St. Elizabeth of Hungary. The iridescent window, created in 1912, shows the saint in a flower garden

### TIFFANY STUDIOS STAINED GLASS INSTALLATIONS

**WHAT** A variety of locations, including homes and churches, with stained glass pieces designed by Louis Comfort Tiffany and his Tiffany Studios

**WHERE** Beecher Mansion, 5475 Woodward Ave.; Christ Church Detroit, 960 E Jefferson Ave.

**COST** Free

**PRO TIP** Visit these locations on a sunny day if you can. While beautiful under any condition, they are particularly impressive when the light hits them just right.

*The Tiffany Studios stained glass found in Detroit depicts saints, floral themes, and more, highlighting Louis Comfort Tiffany's impressive skill with color and composition.*

holding out a portion of her robe that is filled with red and white roses. Like every other aspect of this historic church, the Tiffany Studios piece is stunning in every way possible, from the gentle expression on St. Elizabeth's face to the depth of the red roses. Other Tiffany Studios windows and a chandelier can be found in the city in the Whitney restaurant, David Whitney House, St. Matthews and St. Joseph's Episcopal Church, Cass Community United Methodist Church, Sweetest Heart of Mary Church, and St. John's Episcopal Church.

---

Louis Comfort Tiffany was an innovator with stained glass, one of the first to "paint" the material using opalescent and multihued tones.

# 78 ROW YOUR BOAT

**What Club has the honor of being the oldest rowing organization in continuous existence in the nation?**

Organized on February 18, 1839, the Detroit Boat Club is the oldest organization of its kind in the United States. Established to create a rowing team on the Detroit River, the Detroit Boat Club drew the city's elite to its doors for exercise, socializing, and racing on the water. Being the oldest anything is achievable when you're in a city as old as Detroit, but the Detroit Boat Club has many distinctions beyond its age.

It is also home to the Detroit Boat Crew Club, which heads its rowing program. Sponsored by the Friends of Detroit Rows, the Detroit Boat Club has a nationally ranked crew of rowers, and it offers classes for young and old who are interested in trying the sport. These groups have co-existed within the Detroit Boat Club's Mediterranean-style clubhouse—with its maritime theme, carved seahorses, and reinforced concrete shell—which has graced Belle Isle since December 1901.

The Boathouse has hosted everything from famous bands to swimming championships to Olympic trials. The building had fallen into disrepair following a decline in club membership, issues over membership rights,

## DETROIT BOAT CLUB

**WHAT** A club, rowing group, and building association devoted to the love and pursuit of water sports such as sailing and rowing.

**WHERE** Belle Isle

**COST** Free to visit; membership fees vary

**PRO TIP** Membership is available to the public if you are interested in sailing, rowing, learning any of those sports, and willing to pay the associated fees.

*The Detroit Boat Club is one of the oldest buildings on Belle Isle and is in the midst of a renovation and rejuvenation project.*

and city disinvestment. However, a group called the Friends of Detroit Rowing took over the building's lease from the city and are slowly rehabbing the facilities. Despite all the challenges thrown its way, the Club and its members remain true. Rowers and sailors in the Club's fleet of Flying Scots use the facility almost daily when the Michigan weather is favorable for their turn on the Detroit River, giving the waterways a touch of class with their grace and strength.

---

**The Detroit Boat Club also is the oldest social organization in Michigan, including some of Detroit's oldest families such as the Dibleys, Bateses, Brushes, Farnsworths, and Campaus.**

# 79 THAT DOME LIFE

**Why are there geodesic domes in Southwest Detroit and who built them there?**

There are Detroit landmarks that—much like pop-music singers—can go by a single name, and you know exactly what people are talking about. Examples include Navin, Olympia, or the Depot. You could easily add the geodesic domes on Vernor Highway to that list. Musician Leo Gillis, brother of White Stripes co-founder, and Third Man Records creator Jack White and his wife Parkii are said to have ordered the dome plans for $20,000. With the help of some friends, the couple built them in 1999 on a piece of property near Roosevelt Park at a price of about $90,000.

According to real estate listings, the two domes are four-thousand square feet with open floor plans and attached

## GEODESIC DOMES

**WHAT** Two domes built in the architectural style created by R. Buckminster Fuller located in Southwest Detroit.

**WHERE** 2667 W Vernor Hwy.

**COST** Free to view (The domes were listed at $399,000 when they went up for sale in 2017.)

**PRO TIP** If you're interested, these domes were still for sale and relatively unfinished as of this book's printing.

---

R. Buckminster Fuller, an inventor and engineer, developed the geodesic dome in 1948 as the perfect home style; an example of his Dymaxion residential development is on display at The Henry Ford in Dearborn.

*With their igloo-like shape, the geodesic domes are recognizable to anyone who passes by them.*

garages. "We love this neighborhood, we're from here, and we wanted to make a statement that things are happening here, innovators live here," Gillis told the *Metro Times* in 2005. A geodesic dome gains strength through its construction, dividing a sphere into equal triangles—hence the cut-up look to Detroit's two domes. They are made from steel-reinforced concrete, helping them withstand any weather event or hipster parade. The couple sold the domes after a divorce in 2012 to a development company. For a short time, they were going to be used as event spaces as they are zoned for both residential and commercial use. But they have sat unused for years, waiting for the right owner to renovate and restore them.

# 80 THE STATUE THAT PACKS A PUNCH

**Why is there an eight-thousand-pound fist facing the Detroit River and nearby Canada?**

The larger-than-life statue of Joe Louis's powerful arm is a Detroit landmark that inspires curiosity among any newcomer to the city. Some question what this dramatic installation resembling a fist is doing in downtown Detroit—is it there as an artistic statement or perhaps as a threat to nearby Canada? The story of this memorable piece starts in 1985 when Time Inc., through *Sports Illustrated*, commissioned artist Robert Graham, who specialized in the human form, to create the monument.

The magazine intended it as a gift to the city to honor Joe Louis, its adopted son, and mark the 100th anniversary of the Detroit Institute of Arts as an organization in Detroit. The monument, which is twenty-four feet long, started as a fourteen-inch clay model of "The Brown Bomber" and his famous arm. Using a computer, Graham developed a full-scale steel frame, which he wrapped with wire and covered in clay. The final clay model was divided into eight sections, cast in bronze, and then assembled. It hangs from a pyramidal support of bronze poles, which was fabricated from steel and covered in bronze plates. It rises twenty-four feet above

---

Joe Louis frequently visited Detroit during his celebrated career to see friends in the city's Black Bottom and Paradise Valley districts.

*The Joe Louis fist is a monument to "America's first black hero," a great boxer and a native son of Detroit—Louis's father was originally from the city.*

the street at the intersection of Jefferson and Woodward Avenues. The monument stirred controversy from the start as people complained about everything from its shape to its size to concerns about whether it symbolized Black Power. However, both the creator and its donor said its only purpose was to honor a great city and a great boxer.

## MONUMENT TO JOE LOUIS

**WHAT** A twenty-four-foot bronze statue highlighting Joe Louis, his time in Detroit, and the Detroit Institute of Arts' 100th anniversary within the city.

**WHERE** 5 Woodward Ave.

**COST** Free

**PRO TIP** There is a sidewalk and platform around the memorial, so you can see the fist up close and appreciate its fine details, like the musculature.

# 81 NEIGHBORHOOD ART

**How did a Detroit-raised artist turn his concern over the city's decay into a celebrated art installation?**

Tyree Guyton is a noted painter and sculptor who has works in the Detroit Institute of Arts and other galleries nationwide. Yet to Detroiters, his best-known work is the massive neighborhood art installation known as The Heidelberg Project.

Guyton's mission began when he returned to his childhood neighborhood on Heidelberg Street in the late 1980s only to find it had become a haven for drugs and poverty. Already grieving the loss of three brothers, Guyton responded by taking his grandfather's advice to use his art as a solution to the deepening problems of Detroit. With his family's help, Guyton cleaned the vacant lots on Heidelberg and used some of the cast-off materials to turn abandoned lots and homes into gigantic sculptures, adding objects ranging from dots to dolls to clocks. Guyton's work drew anger, some neighborhood resentment, and plenty of debate. But it also drew visitors, and those visitors brought media attention, awards, and, sadly, arsonists who burned down several homes. Still, Guyton remained true to his goal which was to improve the lives of the people who lived in

## THE HEIDELBERG PROJECT

**WHAT** Artist Tyree Guyton's outdoor art exhibit and community organization that creates conversations about art, the environment, and urban blight.

**WHERE** 3600 Heidelberg St.

**COST** Free (donations welcome)

**PRO TIP** Look but don't touch. Although these are "found" objects, the Heidelberg Project is a work of art that draws thousands of visitors each year.

*For more than thirty years, artist Tyree Guyton has developed The Heidelberg Project along the street where he grew up, hoping the art would heal the neighborhood and, in turn, the city.*

this largely distressed neighborhood, bringing investment to an otherwise blighted street. Guyton, who has been described as an urban environmental artist, was inspired to create The Heidelberg Project in part because of his personal war on the property abandonment that has adversely affected Detroit. By turning his neighborhood into a living indoor/outdoor art gallery, Guyton sparked conversation about Detroit's white flight, real-estate disinvestment, and the city's forgotten neighborhoods. Recently, Guyton and city officials have battled over expanding the Heidelberg Project; the fate of the plan remains uncertain.

---

Recent arsons have destroyed several of artist Tyree Guyton's installations, but the community group that supports the project is slowly rebuilding them.

# 82 RAILROAD TO REHAB

**How did artists, city officials and nonprofit groups come together to transform a former railroad line into a recreational pathway?**

For decades, trains rumbled along the Grand Trunk Railroad line, moving goods from food to raw materials to pharmaceuticals through Detroit to their final destinations. The Dequindre Cut was built twenty-five feet below the street level to eliminate congestion on some of Detroit's busiest thoroughfares. When the railroad stopped using this route in the 1970s, the development was abandoned, and the area became littered, covered with graffiti, and dangerous for people in the neighborhood.

In the late 2000s, the Community Foundation for Southeast Michigan began to reclaim abandoned areas in hopes of creating a connected walkway between cities and landmarks, and the group took an interest in the Dequindre Cut because of its proximity to the downtown and ability to connect key areas of the city. The resulting rehab, which opened in May 2009, serves as a connection between the Riverfront, Eastern Market, and the neighborhoods in between. The greenway, which caters to every kind of pedestrian and traveler on wheels, has a twenty-foot wide paved pathway, which has separate lanes for people and bicycle traffic. To reclaim the space, groups have

---

Late developer and urbanist Tony Goldman described the Dequindre Cut as "one of the most important infrastructure projects in the country," and other cities have copied the idea.

*The Dequindre Cut's artwork, greenery, and separation from the city above makes it an ideal respite from the noise and busy pressures of modern life.*

sponsored additional graffiti by commissioned artists such as Mike Han, Fel3000ft, and others to add curated artwork to the mix already found there. The Dequindre Cut is part of an overall plan for a twenty-six-mile Inner Circle Greenway, which would encircle Detroit and connect neighborhoods to all of the city's many attractions. The Dequindre Cut is currently managed by the Detroit Riverfront Conservancy, a nonprofit dedicated to preserving and maintaining the city's RiverWalk project.

## DEQUINDRE CUT GREENWAY

**WHAT** An urban recreational path that includes some of the finest artwork and graffiti found within Detroit.

**WHERE** 300 River Place South, Ste. 2900

**COST** Free

**PRO TIP** Entrance ramps to the Cut are located at Atwater St., Franklin St., Woodbridge St., Lafayette St., Gratiot Ave., Wilkins St., and Mack Ave.

# 83 A CEMETERY FOR THE AGES

**What is the quietest graveyard in Detroit–mostly because it is surrounded by a massive automotive factory?**

It is Jewish holy ground—with an automotive plant surrounding it. A unique relationship connects Beth Olem, a 2.2-acre, 1,100-grave Jewish cemetery, with its neighbor, a General Motors Corp. manufacturing facility. The story begins in the late 1860s when a Jewish Congregation, Shaarey Zedek, created Beth Olem; the phrase means "house of the world" in Yiddish. It was a cemetery in what was considered the country, and it served as a burial place mostly for middle-class Jewish residents. Chrysler built its Dodge main factory nearby, and its driveway was near the cemetery. Decades later, people began moving to the suburbs and burials slowed in Beth Olem.

By the 1940s, the cemetery sat quietly in a largely Polish community known as Poletown. In the early 1980s, Detroit officials pulled together an area for GM to build a plant, and they set their eyes on Poletown. However, Jewish law as well as Michigan law prohibits the removal of Jewish graves. Shaarey Zedek worked with GM and the city to keep Beth Olem in its original state and location. Beth Olem, which is under the guardianship of Clover Hill Park Cemetery, is open two times a year to allow family members to visit their ancestors. To get in, visitors go through GM security and drive about a mile around the plant until they see an iron arch with rusted letters that reads, "BETHOLEM CEMETERY." A red brick wall surrounds the graveyard, which remains a place of honor and ceremony.

*Beth Olem Cemetery, which is also known as The Smith Street Cemetery, has burials dating back to 1848.*

Beth Olem was the second Jewish burial ground in Detroit; the first was a half-acre area within Elmwood Cemetery established by Temple Beth El.

## BETH OLEM

**WHAT** A Jewish cemetery located within the gates of General Motors Detroit/Hamtramck Assembly plant known as Poletown.

**WHERE** 2500 E Grand Blvd.

**COST** Free

**PRO TIP** Beth Olem opens twice a year for family members and curious visitors from 10 a.m. to 1 p.m. on the Sundays before Rosh Hashanah and Passover.

# 84 UNDER YOUR FEET

**Where can you find one of the world's largest salt deposits?**

The Detroit Salt Mine truly is a city under a city. The mine, which is about twelve hundred feet below street level, has more than one hundred miles of underground roads across about fifteen hundred acres from Detroit to Dearborn to Melvindale. If the mine shaft were a building, it would rank among the world's tallest. Some put the salt deposit's age at around four hundred million years, the result of evaporated oceans and their salty remains. It is likely that Native Americans were the first Detroit residents to discover it, but by 1895 local industries had an eye on mining it for its commercial potential. Opening around 1906, the salt mine is one of the city's oldest and most reliable industries. Parks and neighborhoods built up around it—back then, people had to walk or ride horses on their daily commute—so they wanted to live near where they worked. By 1914, the Detroit Salt Mine was producing eight thousand tons of rock salt each month, mainly for the leather and food processing industries. By 1922, the mine added a second tunnel to boost capacity. Workers once used dynamite to blast the salt out of the mine—in fact, neighbors got used to hearing its regular afternoon reverberations. These days, salt is

---

*To bring in equipment, the Detroit Salt Mine must dissassemble every item and lower it down piece by piece through its narrow second shaft. The equipment is then reassembled in a machine shop below.*

*The Detroit Salt Mine is said to be the largest salt deposit in the world with millions of tons of rock salt.*

## DETROIT SALT MINE

**WHAT** A massive salt mine located below Detroit and several neighboring communities.

**WHERE** 12841 Sanders St.

**COST** Free

**PRO TIP** You can see the outside of the salt mine from a nearby freeway overpass, but you cannot go onto the property as it is a privately held company that does not offer tours.

removed through a huge auger and moved to the surface by a conveyor-belt system. Most of the mine's product is used as road salt, helping communities across the state and the nation remove ice and snow during cold winters. The mine's current owner, Detroit Salt Company and its parent company The Kissner Group, say they produce an estimated 1.7 million tons of rock salt per year.

# 85 A GREAT, LATE MAGICIAN

**What happened to Harry Houdini that resulted in his death in Detroit and what remains of his stay here?**

### HARRY HOUDINI'S DETROIT FUNERAL HOME

**WHAT** The W. R. Hamilton Funeral home is the only remaining link to Harry Houdini's sad demise in Detroit.

**WHERE** 3975 Cass Ave.

**COST** Free

**PRO TIP** Check out the elaborate design and decorations on both the original funeral home and its 1930s addition; they are beautiful despite the home's decay.

Among entertainers, few names have the power or resonance of Harry Houdini. The master magician gave some of his most memorable performances in Detroit, including a death-defying jump from the Belle Isle bridge. Houdini's final trip to Detroit happened in October 1926 when he was set to perform at a theater called The Garrick. A week before, on Oct. 16, 1926, Houdini suffered a blow to the stomach that wounded him. When he arrived in Detroit, he was suffering from acute appendicitis and had a 104-degree fever. Houdini completed his show that night,

When it was in operation, W. R. Hamilton Company served some of Detroit's most industrious entrepreneurs, including the Ford family. Three generations—Henry, Edsel, and Henry II—were prepared for burial at the Detroit funeral home.

*The funeral home—originally the home of Robert and Jennie Brown—and adjacent Art Deco mortuary chapel are now all that is left of Houdini's stay in Detroit in October 1926.*

but collapsed shortly afterward. He was rushed to Grace Hospital for treatment. According to legend, Houdini told his brother, Theo after a week in the hospital "I'm tired of fighting . . . guess this is going to get me." He died on October 31, 1926. Houdini's body was brought to W. R. Hamilton Funeral Company for preparation for his trip home to New York. There was no public viewing of his body while he was in Detroit. Sadly, The Garrick, Grace Hospital, and the Statler Hotel where Houdini stayed during that fateful trip, have all been torn down. All that remains of Houdini's days here is the funeral home, which has fallen into disrepair and needs to be renovated if it is to become a functional building again. But there is something special about this space and the memory of the man who sparked Detroit's sense of mystery, even for a short time.

# 86 MUSIC MAVENS

**Where can you hear some of the world's best musicians in the world's oldest jazz club in continuous operation?**

Baker's Keyboard Lounge is like a cat with nine lives—every once in a while, it threatens to close yet it finds a way to keep its doors open. That is why Baker's has the unique designation as the world's oldest jazz club. The Baker's story begins in 1933 when Chris and Fannie Baker opened their first business as a lunchtime sandwich restaurant. Their son, Clarence, began bringing in jazz musicians in 1934 as a way to entertain the hungry crowds. The music proved such a selling point that Baker's began bringing in regional and national talent to perform. By 1952, Baker's expanded and remodeled to showcase its current Art Deco interior.

One of its most notable decorations is the piano-shaped bar painted with a keyboard motif—those black-and-white keys truly set the tone for the outstanding music heard within. Baker's Keyboard Lounge has hosted the greatest names in blues and jazz, including Ella Fitzgerald, Miles Davis, Oscar Peterson, George Shearing, Sarah Vaughn, Joe Williams, Maynard Ferguson, Cab Calloway, Woody Herman, Dave Brubeck, and Nat "King" Cole. As a result, the Michigan State Historic Preservation Office designated Baker's as a Historic Site in 1986. Its intimate setting—only ninety-nine people can be seated at one time—along with its Steinway pianos, excellent acoustics, and overall style give Baker's the character that makes it a city standout.

---

*The club still displays its original liquor pricelist from 1934, showing the cost of beer at twenty-six cents.*

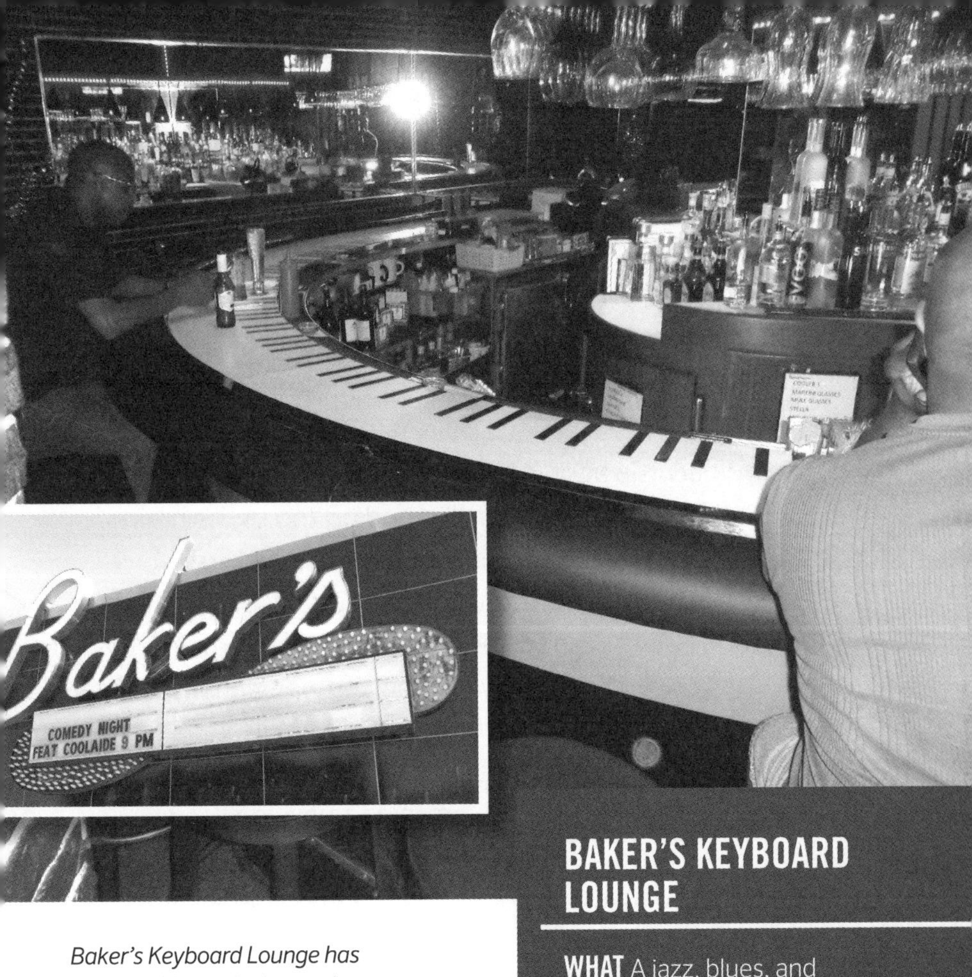


*Baker's Keyboard Lounge has legions of fans who love to be seen at Michigan's jazz hub and Detroit's oldest jazz club in continuous operation.*

## BAKER'S KEYBOARD LOUNGE

**WHAT** A jazz, blues, and bebop mainstay that has the distinction of being the oldest jazz club in continuous operation anywhere.

**WHERE** 20510 Livernois Ave.

**COST** Cover fee plus drinks and dinner

**PRO TIP** Baker's is open for lunch on Tuesdays and usually brings in a jazz singer to perform for its crowd of lunchtime regulars.

# 87 A MOOOVING LANDMARK

**Why is there a giant cow head on top of an empty ice-cream store and how did it get there?**

He was a millionaire. He was a sheriff. And he loved cows. Ira Wilson also was a brilliant marketer for his namesake company, Ira Wilson & Sons Dairy. He founded a dairy in 1930 and became a top milk producer for most of Metro Detroit. This "bovine billboard" stood on top of the main entry point for the dairy at I-94 and the Jeffries Freeway. The fourteen-foot tall tribute to the mighty milk-producing mammal went up sometime in the 1950s and remained there until the early 1980s when the company finally had it removed. Another cow head went up on a Wilson dairy store in 1955 on Detroit's East side.

The Wilson Dairy Stores were said to have delicious selections of candy, baked goods, and ice cream. Although there were multiple locations, only the one at Mack and Lenox had the giant cow head, which soon became a favorite local landmark. The Wilson store closed sometime in the 1960s, and another ice-cream joint tried to take its place. That closed as well, and a barbecue take-out restaurant tried to succeed there. It, too, closed. The cow head stood watch over a vacant storefront until it received some love from Eminem's production crew who spiffed it up for a scene in the 2002 film, *8 Mile*. The building was recently for sale for about $80,000.

---

The cow head had a small part in musician Eminem's movie *8 Mile*. The film crew restored the building so the rapper-turned-actor could shoot a paintball at it.

*The cow head has long stood guard over Detroit, moving from the West side to the East side when it changed owners.*

## GIANT COW HEAD

**WHAT** A large statue of a Borden cow that sits on top of the former Ira Wilson & Sons Dairy Building.

**WHERE** 13041 Mack Ave.

**COST** Free

**PRO TIP** Bring your camera or smartphone because a selfie with a giant cow head is definitely something to brag about on social media.

# 88 PICTURE THAT

**Why are there thousands of Polaroid pictures of everyday Detroiters hanging in a Southwest party store?**

They hang from every visible surface of the Lawndale Market—an estimated ten thousand Polaroid photos of people who have visited this small convenience retailer. For more than three decades, owner Amad Samaan has willingly hung photographs of his customers on the walls of his business. It all started around 1995 when a neighborhood kid saw a picture of the owner's family hanging on the wall. Hoping to join Samaan's grandkids in their photographic fame, the young man asked if his photos could hang in the store as well. With the help of a Polaroid camera, thousands of people have joined in the fun. There are rows upon rows taped to the walls. There are strands of them crisscrossing the store. There are some on the counters, covering the ceiling, tacked to every square inch of space. The faces are of happy times—kids grinning, families pressed together, young people in their prime. These frozen images tell a story of a place and a neighborhood where people recognize one another by face and by name. Samaan, who also is a big fan of Elvis and other Hollywood stars, is glad to have so many customers to remember every time he steps into his business. He even writes "God bless you" on nearly every photo to show just how much he truly cares for Detroit and for the people who shop in his market.

*The owner's kindness to a young customer resulted in a one-of-a-kind display of customers through Polaroid photos.*

Polaroid no longer makes its signature film, so now Lawndale Market depends on its customers to bring in their own photos for the store to hang.

## THE PEOPLE'S POLAROIDS

**WHAT** A photographic display of the thousands of people who have showed up at the Lawndale Market.

**WHERE** 1136 Lawndale St.

**COST** Free (if you bring in your own photo)

**PRO TIP** Make sure to support this business by buying something to eat or drink when you come in to see the pictures or hang one of your own.

# 89 DETROIT'S SYNAGOGUE

**Where is the last known synagogue in Detroit and what happened to the rest?**

Detroit was an engine of innovation, construction, and manufacturing in the 1920s. The city grew by leaps and bounds, and its religious community was just as robust as the population. The city's Jewish community was larger then, and there were dozens of places to worship. The Isaac Agree Downtown Synagogue was established in 1921 to meet the needs of the local Jewish community that lived near the downtown core. As Detroit's population shifted to the suburbs, the city lost its substantial community. As a result, many synagogues closed their Detroit locations and moved to follow their congregations to cities such as Oak Park, Southfield, and West Bloomfield. Due to the shifting trends, Isaac Agree is the last remaining free-standing synagogue in Detroit. It has limited services due to a smaller community and other issues. But the Downtown Synagogue proudly continues to offer weekly Sabbath and High Holiday services, which bring in hundreds of worshippers. It has occupied its easily recognizable four-story building with its signature triangular design and colorful windows since the 1960s. The building is in the midst of a renovation, an increase in programming, and fund-raising efforts to

---

There once were more than sixty synagogues in Detroit proper, and they had architecturally beautiful buildings that are now theaters and other businesses.

*The Downtown Synagogue's goal is to serve as a beacon for the entire Jewish community of Metropolitan Detroit by maintaining an egalitarian synagogue.*

maintain its presence in Detroit. With the January 2017 addition of Rabbi Ariana J. Silverman, the Downtown Synagogue seems well on its way to another century in the city.

## ISAAC AGREE DOWNTOWN SYNAGOGUE

**WHAT** A Jewish worship center that is the last synagogue in Detroit.

**WHERE** 1457 Griswold St.

**COST** Free (donations accepted)

**PRO TIP** If you'd like to tour the facility, the synagogue welcomes visitors who want to learn more about the building as well as the Jewish faith.

# 90 WISHING TREE

**Why did controversial singer and artist Yoko Ono dedicate a "wish tree" to the city of Detroit?**

If you believe wishes can come true, then you need to visit Detroit's official "Wish Tree." This leafy installation occurred in April 2000 when artist Yoko Ono visited Detroit at the behest of local residents Lila and Gilbert Silverman. The couple invited Ono to create something for the city after supporting "Freight Train," one of Ono's works displayed at the Detroit Institute of Arts. The original tree, a ginkgo, was supposed to be both a living sculpture and what Ono called "a symbol of faith in Detroit," according to The Detroit News. A small plaque attached to a boulder next to the tree's location reads: "WISH TREE for Detroit. Whisper your wish to the bark of the tree. yoko ono 2000 spring." The tree became part of what was known then as Times Square Park. In 2009,

### YOKO ONO'S WISH TREE

**WHAT** A tree and plaque devoted to Yoko Ono's faith in the future of the city of Detroit.

**WHERE** Rosa Parks Transit Center

**COST** Free

**PRO TIP** Parking nearby the transit center is scarce, so be prepared to park and walk to see the Wish Tree at its corner location.

---

In addition to Detroit, Yoko Ono installed other "Wish Tree" projects around the United States in cities including Washington, D.C., to encourage the general public to become more involved with art.

*Detroit brought in a new Wish Tree in November 2017 to maintain Yoko Ono's installation of a tree for residents to wish on as they passed.*

the city stepped in again to protect the site and the Wish Tree when it built the Rosa Parks Transit Center. The busy center, where Detroit buses move in and out dozens of times an hour, wasn't the most hospitable site for a tree, and several versions of the Wish Tree died unexpectedly. However, the city added a new linden on the site in November 2017 as part of Mayor Mike Duggan's efforts to plant ten thousand trees in Detroit over a three-year period. With its future shade and comfortable boulder, many passing by the Wish Tree are likely to appreciate Ono's sentiment and the city's investment.

# INDEX